TOM BUCHWALD

BERLIN
Violated city

Vanquished, occupied, walled in

The History of Berlin

With the cooperation of the
Hagen Koch Berlin Wall Archive

SCHIKKUS-VERLAG
In cooperation with Forrest Books (FORBS)
Publishing International, Birmingham – Berlin

First edition in German: 2005
Edition with 198 illustrations

Published by	SCHIKKUS Verlag + Großhandel GmbH & Co.KG
	Nordlichtstrasse 71
	13405 Berlin
	Tel.: 030 – 36 40 77 0
	Fax: 030 – 36 40 77 77
	Internet: www.schikkus.de
	Email: info@schikkus.de
	Produced in cooperation with:
	Forrest Books (FORBS)
	Publishing International Ltd.
	Birmingham – Berlin
Photographs	Ullstein Bilderdienst Berlin
	Berlin Archive
	SCHIKKUS publishing company
	Hagen Koch Berlin Wall Archive
	Tom Buchwald
Translation to English	Alan Moore
Design and Layout	kappisdesign, Berlin
	Internet: www.kappisdesign.de
Printed by	Editorial Fisa Escudo de Oro
	Printed in the EU, autumn 2008
ISBN	978-84-378-2776-6
Legal Dep.	B. 29413-2008

Contents

The division of Germany
the story of postwar Berlin...
the construction of the murderous wall
the human tragedies
that took place in its shadow
many events led up to all this.

This book will take the reader through
shocking episodes from the Cold War
and the Nazi legacy
Berlin came into being, like
a terrifying horror story.

If we dare go back there
we shall briefly visit
the past of this matchless city in which
the generations are reflected in universal history
as in no other great metropolis.

By way of introduction
Rather more than a preface

Berlin, May 1945

An image that requires no explanation. The sight of bombed houses, dead bodies filling the streets and children looking for their
parents, brothers and sisters did not have the same effect on soldiers from the four victorious powers as it did on Berliners who
had managed to survive. These had even more to mourn for than
their dead and the devastated city. Besides the ruins caused by
their mad, murderous lust for power, the Nazis had also left
behind a lack of self-esteem that had hit rock bottom. The "people
of poets and philosophers" had been wakened by the devastating
hail of bombs from a dream that they themselves had woven.
Amid "ghosts" from whose grasp they could not escape in time.
Those who had been able to save their lives and little more were
obliged to admit that they had also lost their historic conscience
under the torturing fire that had left them prostrate. This ending
meant for millions of Germans the beginning of a new drama, a
drama whose high point was reached in Berlin. Whilst some
Berliners enjoyed the unearned good fortune of living in one of
the Western sectors according to the division of the city by the
victorious powers, those caught in the sector occupied by the

Saving more than just life.

A soldier rescues a young
family from amongst the
rubble of their home.

Soviets found themselves witnessing the emergence of another dictatorship, this one German: the German Democratic Republic, founded in faithful imitation of the Stalinist model adopted by the Soviet regime. Under the surface of the events leading up to the construction of the Berlin Wall, preceding the tragedies that befell in its shadow, are hidden a number of causes that go back to much earlier times.

Once upon a time...

Very few people know about the prodigious origins of this city which grew up on the plains during the glacial period, this city that would much later be sacked by people blinded by their desperation, their urgent need to sate themselves on the flesh of hanged men... Berlin, the cosmopolitan city, was still a long way off. And at the same time, so close...
Berlin, a cosmopolitan city: since the early-20th century, for countless artists in all fields the springboard to a successful career; for scientists, the bastion of genius; and for all those with new ideas or something to offer, an attractive, profitable centre of attraction.

Between 1918 and 1933, the ancient metropolis on the banks of the River Spree, once the capital of Prussia, of the Empire, of the Weimar Republic and of "Greater Germany", seemed to all those who visited the city the most interesting and attractive in the world. Berlin was home to more Nobel prize winners than any other city, and was praised as a veritable Mecca by scholars and researchers from the five continents. No other city on earth could boast so many famous doctors, so many renowned artists. None could match Berlin for its theatres, its concert halls, its cabarets, its museums. None had such a brilliant criminal investigation squad, nowhere else were so many films made, so many actors and writers to be found, so many newspapers published, particularly when it came to quickly-printed extras. No other city could offer locals and visitors alike such an exciting nightlife; here, all could enjoy themselves without ceremony, following their own nature, whether this was Babylonian or more bourgeois in its outlook.

In those days...

Even after the Nazis rose to power, right up until the start of the Second World War, Berlin continued to be the "freest" German city. Its nightlife continued unabated, bars never closed, not one cabaret announced its farewell performance. Even jazz, condemned throughout the rest of the empire, could be heard here.

Even homosexuals continued to have their own *East of Eden*, around the Nollendorfplatz. Berlin was to continue acting as a showcase for the German Empire. Countless representatives from the international press resided here, as did the entire diplomatic corps, and when any foreigner came to Germany, their visit always started in the Imperial capital. That is why Joseph Goebbels, Reich minister for propaganda and *Gauleiter*, or governor of Berlin, was so determined to conserve the city's peaceful image (apart from the fact that it later became absolutely impossible to control four and a half million inhabitants as closely as the Nazis would have liked. Even during the final years of Nazi government, many Jews and other persecuted people were able to find a hiding-place in the Imperial capital, managing to survive there).

It happened yesterday...

After the Second World War, Berlin began to arouse interest once more, but this time for very different reasons. For the more than six million visitors to the city every year, Berlin's divided nature was a heart-rending spectacle. Those coming here, whether from West Germany or the rest of the Western world and who could obtain a daily pass to visit the eastern part were equally moved by what they saw in West Berlin, where the tragedies of families cruelly split were reflected in the most gaudy and attractive shop windows.

"And now here is my secret, a very simple secret; it is only with the heart that one can see rightly, what is essential is invisible to the eye."

(*The Little Prince*, by Antoine de Saint-Exupèry.)

For the isolated Berliners and for those who came to the city every year, West Berlin was a matchless biotope in which artists, opportunists, adventurers, drop-outs, gold-diggers and those punished by fatal destiny might prosper, well protected and powerfully sheltered. The atmosphere was most unstable, twisted by repressed resentment, the temperature rising, charged by desperate arrogance. Whilst in the eastern part of the city most Berliners endured their "walled in" condition with resigned submission, clinging to one another to make their situation more bearable, in idyllic West Berlin there were lone wolves everywhere. The two social systems could hardly be more different from one another, though they were two hearts beating inside the same breast. Even today, sixteen years after the fall of the Berlin Wall, they still beat at different rhythms... The Wall lives on.

The children's anger:

Demonstration in Kurfürstendamm avenue, Berlin.

In order to understand Berlin's history, even its most recent past, we need to investigate the historic context. Even until the end of the 1960s, a decrepit, blind faith in authority continued to reign amongst the powers that be in Germany, jealous guardians of their own traditions. This was all completely dismantled by Berlin students in 1967. Rage against the parents shook the Republic. Bloody battles against the police took place in the streets after the authorities had violently suppressed the first peaceful demonstrations, taking illegal measures that led to the death of one student. This youth revolt turned the Republic upside-down, and the results were law reform and abolition, as well as a growing, more deeply-felt understanding of the essence of social life in a democracy.

The desire to repress unpleasant confessions was also manifested on the fall of the Wall. For example, at Checkpoint Charlie, the most infamous border post the world has ever known. In the 1990s, this historic site, through which more people from the GDR escaped than at any other point on the frontier between

East and West Germany, became the plaything of unscrupulous property speculators, and representatives of commemorative movements and associations have now turned it into a forum for mutual insult. On all three fronts, all those who were opposed to anything that might cast doubt on their own lives, or on those of family and friends, twisting the facts or simply erasing them from history. Behind the second front lurked those who refused to confront anyone or anything during the Cold War. Finally, there were those who were able to live comfortably with – and even to make a living from – the mourning and memories of others.

The fact is that, after the first act, an early blooming period in which reunification was made very much a visual event, the political powers that be began to work very much in a solitary way. Final decisions were taken in an improvised manner, without planning, decisions which would now be terribly embarrassing to remember if morality did not depend so much on money and marketing nowadays.

Once the Wall had fallen, it was not long before not enough remained for a decent commemoration to take place. Soon, a great blanket of collective repression and oblivion began to spread over Berlin.

"Peoples of the world, look at this city!" exclaimed Ernst Reuter, mayor of Berlin, in 1951, after the Soviets had cordoned off the Western sectors, threatening their inhabitants with death from starvation.

Nothing should be allowed to be forgotten. The people who lived in the Soviet-occupied sector were walled in for 28 years, 2 months and 27 days. The closely-guarded partition that was built to separate East Berlin and the area around the Brandenburg Gate from the West was 155 kilometres long. The wall itself was 107 kilometres in length, whilst the rest was made up of metal fences and other structures still standing even today. But we cannot say, either, that the people of West Berlin were "free". They lived on an island, surrounded no-go areas and checkpoints. If they tried to get to West Germany through the Eastern zone, they could never be quite sure that they would make it to their destination.

More than 1,100 people died in the shadow of the Wall. Shot by frontier guards, abandoned in the death zone until they bled to death, drowned in border waters or thrown from windows... All this against a backdrop of German history from which no Berliner nor any other inhabitant of the country as a whole could escape with an innocent face. A history of which many, their hands completely clean, their confidence still unshaken, were victims in Berlin when it was freed from captivity under the Nazis. Many lost their lives because their impatience led them to ring out the bells of victory too soon..

About the author

Tom Buchwald was born in Berlin on 2 October 1945, son of the publicist Franz-Richard Buchwald, a social democrat activist who was banned from writing during Nazi times. In May 1945, the Soviets appointed him as director of Berliner Rundfunk (Radio Berlin). Accused of espionage by the US, he was executed at Bautzen prison after a completely unfair trial.

Buchwald Junior, also a journalist and publicist, first became known thanks to his popular science books, after which he caused furore with his cultural projects. He has worked as creative director at FORBS (Forrest Books Publishing International Ltd.) since April 2005.

(www.tombuchwald.de)

Berlin's history lives on in each and every one of us

In Imperial times, Berlin was a flourishing, cosmopolitan city, one which seduced visitors thanks to its unflagging faith in the future.

During the "golden years" of the 1920s, Berlin fascinated the world with its splendour and decadent charm.

The city arose from its ashes after 1945, and during the Cold War fascinated visitors due to the horror it caused.

Now, in the sixth year of the 21st century, finally reunified, the city fascinates due to its stark contrasts.

The city leaves no one indifferent. Berlin forms part of a human history that is repeated again and again, because people, at heart, always remain the same. The German capital is a microcosm of universal events. It moves and is moved like no other.

Visiting this city continues to be an obligation, at once a source of joy and pain and unbound amazement, all sensations felt with urgent immediacy.

May 2005

Tom Buchwald

The Nazi Legacy

18 February 1943
"Do you want total war?"

"I ask you: Do you want total war? If necessary, do you want a war more total and radical than anything that we can even imagine today?" Joseph Goebbels, the Reich propaganda minister, roars out this question on the night of 18 February 1943 before thousands of people who have gathered at the Berlin Sports Palace to hear him. And thousands of voices roar back their fervid affirmation and approbation. It seems that the audience that night is representative of the population. The aim is to give the impression that this theatrical propaganda show is really a popular plebiscite. In his speech, broadcast on the radio, Goebbels poses ten questions to his audience, all of which are answered affirmatively with frenetic applause: "First... I want to ask you: Are you resolved to follow the Führer through thick and thin to victory, and are you willing to accept the heaviest personal burdens?"

"That hour of idiocy! If I had told them to throw themselves off the third floor of the Columbus Haus building, they would have."

(The Reich propaganda minister, Joseph Goebbels, years after his speech at the Sports Palace).

The Nazi Legacy

The other questions demand unconditional obedience and devotion from each individual. They require that each shall be prepared to work hard and give their support for measures against "shirkers and black marketeers" and for sharing the burdens equally between high and low, rich and poor.

1 February 1945
The last mad appeal

Berlin has been turned into a fortress. Soviet troops have reached the Oder. In the Reich capital, the propaganda minister Joseph Goebbels is in charge of organising the defence. More than 700,000, the infirm, children and old men, are sent to the front.

While there's life there's hope...

Berlin 1941: Thousands of Berlin children were born between 1939 and 1945, their fate, like these brothers, born to the Gentzow family Kreuzberg, to start their lives in wartime.

Armed with little more than their ragged, emaciated bodies, they are ordered to throw themselves against the attacking soldiers and tank units. "If my own people fails in this task, I will not shed a single tear. They will deserve their fate."

On Goebbels' orders, courts-martial are empowered to try any type of offence that "endangered the courage and fighting strength of the German people". Since the army is still loyal to him, he addresses this order firstly at enlisted men to compel them to assist in the defence of Berlin, and later at the rest of the civil population, ragged and tattered in body and spirit alike.

A first defence plan is drawn up: "Berlin must be defended down to the last bullet". Four defensive rings are formed, and the civil population is enlisted to built anti-tank barricades and to dig trenches. All these preparations to defend Berlin will turn out to be completely useless. Although the army and the SS muster all available troops in the city, the total is just 94,000 souls, all completely exhausted and extenuated, poorly equipped, many completely untrained.

In hat and tie, forced to enlist with the Volkssturm national German militia.

All those who tried to escape this last call to arms were to be shot on the spot.

February 1945:
Instruction on what women and children should do in the air raid shelters.

"Revenge will come soon", promised the Nazis.

The Nazi Legacy

The civil population, which suffers daily air raids until mid-April, is sick of war. More than 45,000 people, mostly civilians, die in the blanket bombing, many surviving only with serious injury and hundreds of thousands traumatised for the rest of their days.

Friedrichstraße, a world-famous street in its day, in 1900 and after the bombings of 1945.

16 April 1945
The end of the end

Monday, 3 am. The dark sky over the River Oder is lit up by flares. At that moment, 14,600 Soviet cannon open fire from the east bank onto German positions in the Seelow Hills. Two and a half million Red Army troops, most of them expert combatants, well-trained, well-equipped and well-fed, launch an attack on the Reich capital. The final battle has begun.

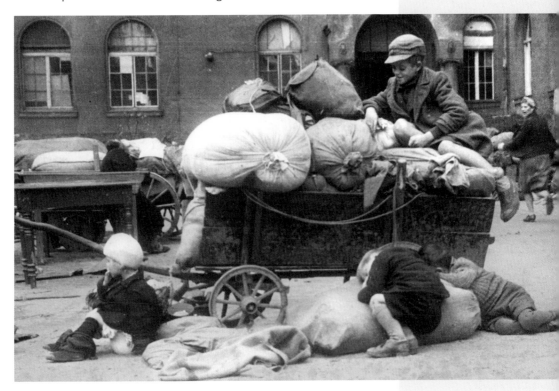

Ignoring threats of the worst punishment, many Berliners attempt to flee from the city. Amongst them, too, are officials from the NSDAP (National Socialist German Workers' or Nazi Party) and civil servants. Those in uniform soon get rid of anything that might enable them to be recognised, as they now also live in fear of the desperate rage of their fellow-citizens.

Refugees from eastern Germany seek protection in Berlin. Exhausted children sleep in the city's streets.

Nonetheless, Goebbels uses all the propaganda means available to give the impression that rescue is imminent and that the German Empire will eventually emerge as the victor on the European battlefield. Many still continue to cling onto hope for such a miracle.

30 April 1945
Hitler commits suicide

Adolf Hitler realises how desperate the situation has become. Maddened by a mixture of bitterness and atrocious fear, he orders the airplane that stands ready to fly him to Berchtesgaden to take off without him. Aware that he will be presented to world opinion as a monster and made to pay for the murder of millions of innocents, he would rather kill himself than fall into the hands of the victorious allied powers.

The Führer-Chancellor commits suicide with Eva Braun, whom he has married just the day before, in the bunker at the new Reich Chancellery. On his orders, their bodies are sprinkled with petrol and burned.

On April 29, Hitler had drawn up his personal and political will and testimony, naming Grand Admiral Karl Dönitz as his heir and proclaiming Dönitz president of the Reich. On January 16, Hitler had returned to Berlin, refusing to abandon the Reich capital, even though Soviet troops had launched a direct attack on it on April 16, as he remained certain that the city would eventually be freed. From his bunker he sends out nonsensical and often con-tradictory orders attempting to lead his armies even as they disin-tegrate. But he is by now the leader of nothing more than a ghost army.

The liberation of Berlin in which he had trusted failing to materialise, Hitler orders that the defence of the city should continue until the bitter end. On April 20, Hitler's 56th birthday, the inner circle that still governs the Third Reich meets for the last time in the Führer's bunker. Those present include Hermann Göring, Hitler's right-hand man, Heinrich Himmler, SS commander in chief, and Joachim von Ribbentrop, minister of foreign affairs. Most leave Berlin that same night. Only Martin Bormann, Hitler's personal secretary, and Joseph Goebbels, minister of propaganda, stay beside their leader. When Göring telegraphs on April 23 to ask whether he should take over as leader of the Reich since the Führer refuses to leave a Berlin now practically in a state of siege, Hitler orders the Reich Marshall placed under arrest.

Hitler receives the news that Heinrich Himmler has gone behind his back and contacted the Western Allies to try to negotiate a "special peace" with them. It is likely that the disappointment he suffers due to Himmler's "betrayal" is what finally leads him to commit suicide.

A photograph of Hitler, shortly before his suicide in the Chancellery gardens.

Published 23 March 1945 in the last edition of the newspaper Die Deutsche Wochenschau.

Moments before the Führer's suicide, Joseph Goebbels takes his wife and children to the bunker to die with him. The children are murdered by their mother, who gives them potassium cyanide, and the couple commits suicide.

The bodies of Goebbels and his wife, Magda, after their suicide in the Chancellery gardens.

2 May 1945

Berlin surrenders to the Red Army

At dawn, General Helmut Weidling, commander of the Berlin Defence Area, under the orders now of Red Army Commander-in-Chief General Vasily Ivanovich Chuikov, delivers the order to all remaining German troops to surrender. Although this order is immediately broadcast all over the city by loudspeakers mounted on Soviet vehicles, military operations continue at some points until May 3, when General Weidling personally intervenes.

And so the Battle for Berlin came to an end after 16 days' fighting. It had begun on April 16, when the Soviets broke through the German defensive lines in Küstrin and Guben, on the banks of the Oder, and two advance columns led the assault on the capital.

Nearly one million Soviet soldiers squared up against defensive forces comprising just 94,000 poorly-equipped, hungry and demoralised men. Just five days after the offensive began, the Soviet artillery had the perimeter of Berlin within range. At that same moment, the first Red Army advance guard units reached the outskirts of the city to the north and northeast.

The Nazi Legacy

On the day of Hitler's suicide, the Soviet flag was raised over the Reichstag building.

On April 22, Soviet troops enter Weissensee and Pankow. Having taken Köpenick, the Red Army conquers Zehlendorf, Tempelhof and Neukölln. Two days later, the Reich capital is completely surrounded.

The raped city

Suddenly, silence reigns over Berlin. A deafening silence. Many believe they still hear the scream of bombs getting ever louder over their heads... but bombs no longer rain down... no more grenade blasts can be heard ...

Amid this silence, many see their first Russian. He pops out suddenly from somewhere and is suddenly there, very close. In a street where practically nothing remains but ruins. Where there are people stooping down to bury the bodies that lie everywhere, or dragging rotting corpses from the mountains of rubble to get them out of sight, carrying them away on rusty old wheelbarrows before the children come back into the streets.

They see him before them, how he looks around cautiously, advancing step by step. Small, strong, worn, tired and dirty. Machine gun in one hand, he works his way along the street, always careful to stay under cover. He does not look like a victorious warrior, rather one who has managed to escape with his life once more. At first sight, he can hardly be distinguished from the defeated, apart from his uniform and his gun.

Then, suddenly, everything changes. Soviet soldiers enter the city en masse. Now they know that they are the victors, that the battle for Berlin has come to an end. From now on, they begin to seek out women. They look for them everywhere. They enter homes, search basements. Later, eye-witness statements will describe how they raided even hospitals, including the Elisabeth Krankenhaus in Lützowstraße. Years later, a scrub nurse, a deaconess who served there along with other sisters, was able to find words to describe the unimaginable:

"The night before, operations were still being carried out in the light of burning buildings. All the next day, seriously wounded people kept pouring into the hospital. Around ten at night, terrible screams began to be heard from the rear wing. I heard shooting and hand grenade explosions. I went out into the corridor. Wounded people were crawling along the floor, their bandages in tatters, climbing up the stairs: the Russians are here!

...Suddenly, the room I was in became filled with nurses. They kneeled and began to pray. Soldiers in uniforms the colour of earth came in and dragged some of them out. I ran into the next room, then the next, opening one door, then another...

The grenades were getting closer, some exploded in the hospital itself. Suddenly, the smell made me realise that the building was on fire. I sprinted through the nurses' rooms. The Russians were everywhere, dragging nurses and patients violently along with them, ripping off their clothes, pouring liquor over them, shooting them against the wall. Then they barricaded the doors so that their comrades could not enter and take their place..."

German prisoners of war were marched to Berlin.

The German soldiers felt no sense of shame.

The abuses committed by the Soviet troops greatly tarnished their act of liberation. At least that is how the one in ten women raped by the Russians in Berlin saw things.

The Nazi Legacy

...I don't know how I managed to get out of the hospital and enter the house adjoining it, how I survived that night by hiding in the basement. The next morning I went back. There were patients and nurses only in some of the hospital wings. The Russians weren't interested in them any more. They were busy in the nearby houses. But in the parts of the hospital where the Russian soldiers had raped the nurses there was now a mass of smoking beams and hot rubble.

... Later, as the work of clearing this away went on, we found the metal bed frames and the charred bodies, terribly contracted, locked together. The holstered belts and the shoes told us that the Russians, in their drunkenness, had burned along with the women they had dishonoured".

The Russians were busy in the nearby houses. Yes, during those first days after the fall of Berlin, there was hardly a house where they were not "busy". Women tried to disguise themselves, blackening their faces to try to appear old and ugly. Some painted ghastly-looking sores on their faces or disguised themselves as men. Rifle butts were heard banging against doors constantly as Red Army soldiers burst into homes, seizing the prettiest women, even twelve-year-old girls. One soldier would stand guard outside the door, and the inhabitants of the house could hear the chilling screams for help as their womenfolk were raped.
Few Russians bothered to remove their clothes before committing their crimes. The rapes later reported made it clear that none cared who might be watching. Many women were violated before their husbands and children.

Years, often decades, had to pass before the victims could talk about their fate. Many prefer to remain anonymous, some fear that their husbands might not forgive them for having been raped, not just once, but ten, twenty times, and not by one, two or three Russians, but by dozens taking turns over their ravaged bodies.

But the opposite was also true at times. Many Russians behaved in a friendly way. Some seemed to be good, innocent people. They knocked at doors and looked in puzzlement at the toilet bowl, which they thought was the place to wash fruit and potatoes. They were amazed by everything they saw in Berlin homes, by the lamps and, particularly, by the watches, which they often made off with.
In the street, they pounced on people for their clothes. Many Berliners watched as their neighbour, husband or friend was forced to take off their overcoat because a soldier preferred it to

his own. "Your coat, me your coat!" they shouted, waving their pistols. When they got home, those persuaded to make the exchange might, with luck, find that the pockets of the Russian's overcoat contained a watch or a handful of gold jewellery.

No single skin colour, no single language, no single nationality...

Nikolai E. Bersarin
A blessing for Berlin

The commander-in-chief in Berlin, surrounded by Soviet writers and correspondents. On the left, Alexander Prokofjew, on the right, Alexander Besymenski.

A degree of order was soon restored amongst the Russian soldiers after the fall of Berlin. The Soviet commander in chief in the city, Nikolai E. Bersarin, who soon became enormously popular amongst the people of Berlin, meted out Draconian punishments against all those found guilty of crimes against the civilian population. And when the first terrible images from the freed concentration camps were published, people began to understand that the beast which human beings carry inside them has no single colour, no single language, no single nationality. Nor can it be killed so easily.

Out of the ruins once more

Headscarf tied firmly. There is work to do.

The mortar has to be removed from bricks so that they can be reused.

May 1945
The "Trümmerfrauen"

Terrible chaos continues to reign on the streets. The children play amongst the ruins, returning home with Nazi medals, old masks, machine guns and swastikas. Their horrified parents are still afraid that the Russians might shoot them if they see these objects from a world that no longer exists.

Work to clear the rubble begins all over the city. The Berlin streets are piled high with this rubble, sometimes metres deep. Most of the work is done by the Trümmerfrauen, or "rubble women", who begin the task armed with the most rudimentary equipment, buckets and spades. Stones from walls and iron and wooden beams are salvaged from the rubble.
(A salary of 72 Pfennigs per hour for the coming months is established in June 1946, as is the punishment for those who refused to work, who do not receive a ration book).

An appetite for the dead:

Horses dead from exhaustion are welcome treats. A man drags part of a dead horse along the pavement.

13 May 1945
The forbidden black market

Distribution of the first ration cards since the end of the war is announced. The Berlin population is divided into five groups of people to be fed: those doing heavy, manual work, the so-called "deserving academics" and artists, receive the lion's share. Those with no profession are allotted the lowest rations. Average intake amongst Berlin's inhabitants is around 1,400 calories a day. The food handed out is not enough for survival. Those who cannot find some other source of nutrition will end up dying of hunger. The city people start to discover the black market, but the victorious powers immediately ban all such activity. Nonetheless, even occupation soldiers do business on the black market. The most valuable commodities are cigarettes, which cost more than the 10 marks a "rubble woman" earns a day for just one. Practically anything can be found, though at scandalously high prices. It is in Münzstrasse in the centre of Berlin that this forbidden market most flourishes and booms. Many nations join together here. Russian and American soldiers receive watches in exchange for the clothes, pork meat and butter that the citizens need. "Hurrah! We're still alive!" This is the phrase that best expresses the sentiments that reigns amongst the people of Berlin in those days and weeks. Public life begins in the city once more. Many Berliners enjoy the first spring sunshine from the pavement cafés, which have opened their doors to the public once more.

A couple of salted herring in the Central Market to fight off the daily pangs of hunger.

...and on the pavement
opposite the same
Kurfürstendamm.

15 May 1945
At last, there are newspapers again

The Soviet army had occupied the German capital even before
the Allied troops entered the city. Their press officers edited and
immediately approved the first newspapers published in Berlin
after the war. The first issue of *Berliner Zeitung* came out in May
1945. Soon after, the Allied advance troops establish their own
mouthpiece: *Der Berliner* (later to become the *Telegraf*) begins to
roll off the presses in Wilmersdorf in the British section.
First edition: Thursday, 2 August 1945, 20 Pfennigs. The caption
under a large photograph: important Soviet decoration for Allied
commanders, who hold glasses of champagne. Below, headlines,
news, reports. Ultimatum to Japan: surrender or destruction.
Tokyo refuses to capitulate, more than 300 flying fortresses drop
2,200 fire bombs. US losses since the start of the war now

standing at 1,058,842. Local news: "Berliners crying out for insulin", "Nicotine breeds thieves". Post office worker Friedrich W. sentenced to two months in prison for stealing cigarettes from parcels. Fifty years old, twenty-three in the post, no previous convictions, a family man, affected by the war ...

Brave reporters get back on the job. You have to work hard if you want to get on the front page. It is important to pick up everyday sensations to help Berliners to recover a feeling of "normality". By 1946, no fewer than 15 newspapers are being published in Berlin. There is the *Kurier* in the French sector, the *Spandauer Volksblatt* and the *Sozialdemokraten* in the British sector and the *Tagesspiegel* (which still exists, even today) in the US sector. Anyone interested can also read and even subscribe to the new dailies coming out in the Eastern sector. The variety is rich and revealing. Thanks to it, those living in West Berlin begin to receive wind of the new "air" beginning to sweep through the Soviet zone before the rest of Germany learns about such developments.

4 May 1945
Intrigue concerning the legendary RiaS begins

On this day, the Berliner Rundfunk begins transmitting from the HAUS DES RUNDFUNKS (House of Radio) in Masurenallee Avenue, inaugurated on 22 January 1932. Opposite stands the radio tower, which entered into service in 1926. Here, the Soviets are in control, as they had taken over the building as soon as they entered the city.

(The North Americans, the British and the French are also occupied in organising their own radio stations. Amongst Berliners, the eventual favourite is AFN. Its first broadcasts are not far off: the radio station's first programmes will be aired on 4 August 1946).

The Western Allies do everything in their power to influence Berliner Rundfunk in some way but, though in theory ultimate power rests with the city magistrate, in practice it is also controlled by the Soviets, who turn the station into a propaganda weapon. The Western powers have to make a *Voice of the Free World* ring out as soon as possible, but it is not so easy. Firstly, they must find the necessary "sounding boxes" to create the programme, and which is used by Berliner Rundfunk. The broadcasting director, Franz-Richard Buchwald, a journalist who formerly worked on the *Vossische Zeitung*, a newspaper banned by the Nazis, is not happy with the political line imposed on him. That the Soviets appoint him director in late-April 1945 is the price he will have to pay for the prohibition from publishing that he suf-

Franz-Richard Buchwald

Journalist and publicist, a social-democrat active during Nazi times who was banned from writing. Joined the resistance and went underground in 1942. First director of Berliner Rundfunk radio after the war. Condemned by the communists of "spying for the RiaS" (German name for the American sector radio station), he died in mysterious circumstances at Bautzen prison...

fered as an active social democrat during Nazi times and for helping opponents of the regime and those persecuted by the Nazis to escape by providing them with false papers. During the de-Nazification investigations, Jewish survivors issued Buchwald with a certificate of good conduct. With such a personal background, it is no surprise that he cannot go along with the Soviet way of doing things, and he secretly enters into negotiations with United States officials, allowing himself to be persuaded to switch sides. On 21 November 1945, Colonel James Westerfield of US headquarters issues an order to establish a radio station in the American sector. Armed with his "apprentice" and future star, Hans Rosenthal, and the basic recording material necessary to begin, Buchwald launched broadcasts by DIAS (the German initials for wire radio broadcasting in the American sector).

(Starting 7 February 1946, DIAS is received by telephone connection. At first, programmes are broadcast in precarious conditions from rooms provisionally equipped for the purpose on the third floor of the telephone company headquarters in Winterfeldtstrasse street in Schöneberg. DIAS is on the air every day, from 5 pm to midnight, staffed only by Germans, though under strict American control. The station, under the direction of Franz Wallner-Basté, broadcasts news from all over the world as well as concerts, popular music and the first big band recordings. Indeed, the American masters enabled records practically unknown in Germany to be heard over the wires. It is from these shaky beginnings, then, that the legendary RiaS is finally launched on 5 September 1946. At last, all Berlin could listen to the "free voice of the free world" by radio aerial. Having fulfilled its mission for some 45 years, RiaS finally closed down after German Reunification. Now, Deutschlandfunk broadcasts from the building in Kufsteiner Strasse formerly used by RiaS).

Franz-Richard Buchwald paid a high price for his convictions: he was persecuted by Soviet Secret Services, arrested in West Berlin's Köpenick district, tortured and sentenced to twelve years in prison as a "spy for RiaS" after a show trial presided over by "bloody" Hilde Benjamin, the "Red Guillotine". In "Yellow Misery", as the infamous Bautzen prison is known, the principal mission was to ensure the "elimination of enemy ideologies" amongst inmates. This physical and moral destruction of "class enemies" (of the GDR) was perpetrated to extremes at Bautzen II, where the political prisoners were held. This is where Franz-Richard Buchwald died just months after he was interned there in circumstances that have never been made clear. The truth is, he was sentenced to death along with many other Cold War victims during the post-war period.

Many people gave their lives for the Voice of the Free World.

Hans Rosenthal, first radio star in postwar Berlin.

Out of the ruins once more

5 June 1945
Berlin is divided into four sectors

In a holiday villa in Wendenschloss, in the suburb of Köpenick, the commanders-in-chief of the Allied occupation force, "in view of the defeat of Germany", sign a declaration by which the four victorious powers take over state powers. The signatories, still enjoying friendly relations, are: General Dwight D. Eisenhower (USA), Field Marshall Bernard L. Montgomery (Great Britain), General Jean-Joseph de Lattre de Tassigny (France) and Marshall Georgij K. Schukow (USSR).

The powers also sign an agreement dividing Germany into four occupied zones and establishing the Allied Control Council has the highest governing body in the country.

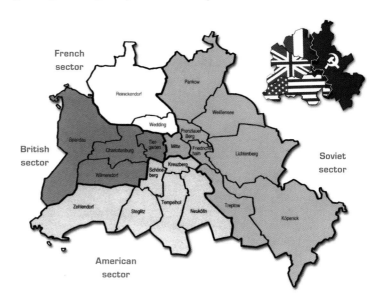

The four sectors

Berlin is the only German city to be divided into four sectors. The Allies had already reached an agreement on this point much earlier, on 12 September 1944, embodied in the so-called London Protocol.

On May 8, the day of capitulation, Berlin is occupied only by Soviet troops. It is agreed that British and American forces should not advance towards their assigned sectors of the city until July 1. In exchange, the Western Allies hand over areas they have conquered in Central Germany to the Soviets (if Berlin had not been established as a joint occupation zone, areas like Thuringia and Saxony would have formed part of free Germany).

Out of the ruins once more

Summer 1945:

Russians and North Americans with German Frauleins, here still joined fraternally by the joy of victory.

The inter-allied military command in Berlin begins its work in the district of Dahlem. On July 30, the Occupation commanders-in-chief meet for the first time at US headquarters in Dahlemer Clayallee, agreeing to establish a French sector in Berlin. As a result, France takes control of the Wedding and Reinickendorf districts.

7 August 1945

Hiroshima destroyed by atomic bomb.
Berlin needs coal

Newspaper readers learn of a terrible event: on August 6, the first atomic bomb is dropped, with explosive power equivalent to 12,500 tonnes of dynamite. This is power impossible to imagine, even by Berliners still traumatised by the devastating Allied bombing of their city.
More than ten square kilometres – the entire centre of Hiroshima – has been completely destroyed, razed to the ground, and, according to Tokyo radio, every living thing in this area, people and animals, has been flattened by the violent expansive wave, or charred to a cinder by unimaginable heat (note: there is no news as yet about radioactivity – an unknown concept to most at the time – and its terrible consequences, nor about the painful deaths many would suffer many years later. Few readers can have failed to wonder how close Germany and, particularly, the Reich capital, Berlin, had been to suffering an attack of this kind).
Everyone in Berlin who has survived the war is glad just to be alive. That day, the sun shines brightly down on the field of rubble that is one a busy, aromatic, splendid cosmopolitan city. The

slightest breeze raises huge clouds of dust. The people fervently hope for rain, but instead another spreading rumour sends a shiver of fear through the population: panic follows the news that there will not be enough coal for the city to get through the winter. As always, the world over, the greatest fear is the one closest to home.

30 August 1945
Allied Control Council established

On 9 June 1945, the commander-in-chief of the Soviet Army of Occupation in Germany, Marshall Georgij K. Schukow, had announced, as "Order Number 1", the creation of the Soviet Military Administration (SMAD). The task given to SMAD is to guarantee "control of conditions imposed under the unconditional capitulation" and to "administer to the Soviet army of occupation in Germany" within the Soviet-occupied zone. The Allied Control Council, on which all four victorious powers are represented, is also established.

First meeting of military governors (from left to right):

Montgomery (Britain)
Schukow (Soviet Union)
Eisenhower (USA)
Koenig (France)

5 October 1945
Economic miracle in Berlin's "Alex"

In Alexanderplatz, the vitality of the Berlin people takes on a very different form to that which can be seen in the elegant cafés on Kurfürstendamm or in the now reopened cabarets and nightclubs. The loudspeakers of Berliner Rundfunk resound around the square, but even they cannot silence the cries of the travelling tradesmen, for the "big mouth" of the Berliners has returned there once more. A barrel organ plays in the centre of a group of people who crowd around stalls hurriedly put up to sell lipstick, nail varnish, hair lotion, face cream... Berlin women dressed in colourful summer clothes that they have made for themselves. They are not the only ones who think they look "good enough to eat". The year's first fur coats, still dusty, are seen. Nonetheless, most people wandering around the square are dressed in the worn and dusty clothes that comprise their uniform in the work of clearing the rubble; their homes are the ruins of what were once houses.

Shopkeepers do a roaring trade: tap handles, egg boxes, hair tongs, tins of food... The first shoeshine boys appear. For a coin or two, they clean anything the customer cares to place under their brushes. They make their own polish. The recipe depends on who is asking: an imperial secret or "Old English". "I have expanded my business, now it is a working firm. I have got four workers and an accountant", says one with a strong Berlin accent. And so what if the core of his business empire is a cripple who sells postcards he paints himself in West Berlin... "That's what sells, I tell you. The Americans feel sorry for cripples", he says, shaking his head. And his company assets also include a set of scales on which at least 500 people weigh themselves every day to see whether they have put on a few ounces. "It needs mending. It doesn't work very well".

Alexanderplatz before it was destroyed.

Out of the ruins once more

...In sackcloth and ashes, and home-sewn.

Berliners have always somehow managed to get by, even managing to look their best in adversity.

Here, the missing father's clothes are altered to fit his son.

A small economic miracle worthy of pride and that will quickly grow to enormous proportions. Just like the smaller-scale miracle that, here, sits on a wooden chair, her back bent, before whom stands someone "better off", tapping away with the hammer of economic recovery. But just a few paces away, the door of opportunity is open to all. A young girl sells tobacco seeds, her shop sign a huge tobacco leaf. Potential growers are informed about the huge profits that can be made. All they need is a balcony. Berlin is booming. One might say, the city is on the Autobahn to new fame and glory. No one can stop her... At least here, in the "Alex", just to the left of the entrance to the Berolina building.

14 January 1946

The rubble field is cleared

The local authority responsible for construction and housing presents its report: the estimated costs for removing all the rubble from the city is 1,450 million *Reichsmark* (Imperial Marks). The figures show that some 12,000 homes have been repaired by 14 January 1946. At the end of the war, one-tenth of Berlin's 250,000 buildings had been totally destroyed and a further one-tenth are so damaged that there is no question of reconstruction. Some 70% had suffered damage of some kind. When the war started, in 1939, there are around one and a half million homes in the city, of which just 800,000 remained in 1945. As more than one person lived in practically all these homes, a large number of Berliners had been affected by the bombing. To this must be added the incalculable damage suffered by factories and roads. Around 85% of all bridges had been destroyed. The cost of repairing the destruction caused by the war in Berlin is estimated at more than 80,000 million *Reichsmark*.

There are not enough machines and tools to carry out the work of clearing the rubble. Above all, though, there is a lack of workers. For this reason, as occurred in other devastated German cities, women of all ages are required to go to work by decrees issued in spring-summer 1945. The rule continues to stand: those who will not help with clearing the rubble will not receive a rations card. The "rubble women" continue to receive 72 Pfennigs for each day worked, the same as men similarly employed. Despite the fact that more than 34,000 people are taken on for this work, the lack of machinery means that progress is slow indeed, and it is estimated that the task will take between 20 and 25 years to complete. Rubble-clearing is not mechanised until 1947.

The first free elections: work or starve!

Rubble clearing work

(from the TV documentary *The Last Battle*, 2005)

29 January 1946
Free beer after North American captivity

Official liberation day. The mayor of Zehlendorf surprises those "liberated" with a barrel of beer. Servicemen recently returned to civil life continue to wear their black-dyed drill jackets bearing the letters PW (Prisoner of War) in white on the back, and which they are not allowed to remove. For this reason, they wear them inside-out. Beer is needed, for the 160 men, all those still held out of the more than 400 German soldiers made prisoners by the Americans, and for whom the return is a saddening event. Some are far from their homes, whilst others search for their bomb-damaged houses and others can barely make out where their streets used to stand, before they were completely razed to the ground. Many seek in vain for their wives, children, parents, friends... The homeless are taken to a hut in the former Argentinische Allee prisoner of war camp in Zehlendorf. There, they somehow find the strength to join the workforce, and the American occupation headquarters employs them as building workers or truck drivers.

9 April 1946
A new university is founded in West Berlin

The name of the former Charlottenburger Chaussee Polytechnic School (at what is now June 17 Street) is changed to that of Technical University. In his opening speech, the mayor and president of Berlin, Arthur Werner, stresses the future objectives and requirements of West Berlin's first university: "The recently-established Technical University must work not only to foster specialist knowledge and skills amongst future generations of German technicians, keeping abreast of world progress, but also to infuse this specialist knowledge in the fertile, inspiring mother earth of a wider personal development..."
(In 1967-68, the world saw that this admonishment had been followed to the letter: one of the main sources of the Berlin student revolt, which shook the whole Republic, is precisely here, at the Technical University).

21 April 1946
Founding of SED divides SPD

The SPD and KPD unification assembly begins. The assembly decides the formation of the Socialist Unity Party of Germany (SED, according to its German acronym). Already, in December 1945, the executive councils of the SPD and the German Communist Party (KPD, according to its German acronym) had agreed to unify their two parties within the territory occupied by the Soviets). The delegates from the recently-founded SED approve the new party's statutes and pass a resolution establishing its objectives. Otto Grotewohl (SPD) and Wilhelm Pieck (KPD) are appointed as presidents. In the western sectors, the SPD had voted against joining the KPD. Thus it is that a split comes about in the Berlin SPD.

Late-April 1946

Outrage in Berlin. Adulterated penicillin dealers arrested

Apart from political developments, those trying to get rich quick also make the headlines. A particularly unpleasant racket is discovered. The people of Berlin had never before been so enraged. The shortage of medicine had been exploited in the most scandalous, shameful way. A gang of ten Berlin criminals had attempted to make 150 million marks from selling adulterated preparations. American and British police arrest the seven men and three women.

The 26-year-old manufacturer, Peter D. of Zehlendorf, and his accomplices, all with experience in the pharmaceutical and cosmetic industries, had flooded the black market with their products. The basic ingredients in the mixture sold as penicillin are face powder, glucose and atebrin. The band charged 15,000 *Reichsmark* for an ampoule of this stuff. They had purchased nine boxes containing 20,000 ampoules of glucose mixture from an army warehouse when this was cleared, at a price of 7 Marks per unit. They used nail polish remover to take off the old labels, replacing them with false labels supplied by a printer, 66-year-old Max P., of Neukölln. The vials are then sold on at a price of 3,000 Marks to intermediaries who added their own 500% mark-up. A trade as lucrative as it is murderous.

28 June 1946

First DEFA film made

After the invasion, the Allies had requisitioned the empire's cinematographic heritage and resources. Around 70% is in Soviet-occupied territory, much of it in Babelsberg. The huge film production site became the headquarters of a company set up in May 1946, Deutscher Film AG (DEFA), whose first feature, "Die Mörder sind unter uns" (*The Murderers Are Among Us*) is the cinema's first postwar reaction against the Nazi terror.

DEFA film (1946). *The Murderers Are Among Us*

Hildegard Knef in her first starring role, alongside Ernst Wilhelm Borchert.

Out of the ruins once more

DEFA produces other successful films, but these promising beginnings come to nothing once the GDR is established and the SED imposes very strict directives over film production, stifling any criticism of the party's political evolution at birth.

The Nuremberg trials against the leading war criminals (poster).

16 July 1946
Hitler's lieutenant living in Berlin

The war criminals sentenced to jail by the International Tribunal in Nuremberg are transferred to Berlin, to the Allied Prison in Spandauer Wilhelmstrasse. The "star" prisoners are the Führer's lieutenant, Rudolf Hess, the economy minister, Walther Funk, and the German Navy commander-in-chief, Erich Raeder. The group also includes the minister of armaments, Albert Speer, the leader of Hitler Youth, Baldur von Schirach, the former foreign affairs minister, Konstantin Freiherr von Neurath and Grand Admiral Karl Dönitz, appointed as Hitler's successor after the Führer's suicide.

When the airplane from Nuremberg lands at Berlin-Gatow, the war criminals board a bus with darkened windows to be taken to the Allied Prison. The prison, built in 1881, is vacated to make room for these inmates by an Allied high command order issued in October 1946, after which the victorious powers took over its running. The Allies thereafter take monthly turns to guard the prisoners.

Late-July 1946
Dad's "Hottentot music"

One day, father is turning the dial to find some good popular music. Suddenly, shockwaves run through him. On 211 metres long wave, he has found one of the first programmes broadcast by the US station AFN (American Forces Network). The network immediately became the favourite amongst young Berliners.
Father had never heard this music before. For him, it is "jungle music". What he heard as warbling and grunting is, in fact, jazz and, later, rock 'n' roll music. It is through these new sounds that Berlin youth begins to rebel against their elders. Needless to say, US soldiers also depend heavily on the programmes broadcast from Dahleme Podbielskiallee. Though far from home, AFN brought a little bit of home to them. Disc jockeys like the legendary Wolfman Jack would soon become cult heroes and genuine stars.

15 August 1946
CARE parcels against the pangs of hunger

Berlin is struck by famine. US private aid gets under way through CARE (Cooperative for American Remittances to Europe). Money donated by this North American charity organisation is sent to the city in the form of standard food parcels and to organisations on the ground, which distribute the aid to needy people in all sectors. With the economic aid provided under the Marshall Plan, CARE parcels form an essential component of the support and assistance the United States gives, not only to Western Europe as a whole, but to West Germany and Berlin in particular. Since the end of the war, few places have depended on outside aid as much as Berlin. Three days after the Western Allies occupied the three western sectors of the city, the Soviet commander-in-chief Soviet had backed out of his promise to provide food for the whole of Berlin. It is impossible for zones occupied by the Soviets to send food to the rest of Berlin due to the shortages they themselves are facing.

Care parcels, a pleasant surprise for Berlin families and a need to ensure that many did not starve to death.

21 August 1946
Playing children find explosive devices

The police drive around the city with loudspeakers mounted on their vehicles, warning the population. Ammunition and explosive devices left over from the days of battle still lurk amongst the rubble, in parks and in gardens. Adults should look after their children when they let them out to play, as terrible accidents can be caused by material that could explode at the slightest touch. A seven-year-old girl loses her forearm, a boy of nine his foot. The police have been destroying as much of this perilous ammunition as they can since the end of the war in 1945. From August 1945 on, in the American sector alone, 30,000 units of artillery ammunition, 750,000 infantry rounds, 1,000 incendiary bombs and 280 mines are deactivated, exploded safely or otherwise rendered inoffensive.

5 September 1946
Berliners listen in to first RiaS broadcast

The RiaS takes to the airwaves at last! This is the American sector radio station, a free voice in the free world. Today, at 15:00 hours, broadcasting begins with a speech by the mayor and president, Dr. Werner, who welcomes the initiative, declaring that, since the entry of the occupying powers, Berlin has become an international city whose atmosphere has taken on new colour thanks to the launch of a radio station controlled by the North Americans.

The first day's programmes feature, apart from excellent music, the famous novelist Erich Kästner and the actor and cabaret artist Werner Fink. Kästner, who left Berlin in March 1945, had returned to the city that same morning from Munich. The first thing he did is to go to his old apartment in Charlottenburg. Reaching the studio at around noon, he mentions that that his bath is still hanging from the wall of the devastated building. The sound engineer then indicates that it is time to start broadcasting, and Kästner takes the microphone. Introducing the title of his programme to the people of Berlin as *Interview with Myself*, he begins as follows: "You know more or less what an interview is. People come that you have never met before and that you hope you will never see again, and you ask them stupid questions. The replies are things that absolutely no one is interested in." Kästner then proceeds to interview himself.

13 October 1946
British free first group of Berlin prisoners

Women with long faces and thin legs and arms, wearing worn summer coats, stand freezing cold beside girls in their warm fur coats. The square outside Grunewald station is buzzing with life. Men, women and children are all standing there, waiting, agitated, disordered. Small groups form, endless, animated discussions take place.

Two days earlier, on the Friday, the *Telegraf* had published lists of those taken prisoner by the British who are expected to be returned home. And now they wait. Many are worried: "What will he look like, how will I recognise him?"

The dolly birds, however, have other concerns: "Will he just look at my fur coat without saying anything? Would it have been better to wait for him in sackcloth and ashes in the hope that he would not suspect later on?"

The arrival of 617 people has been announced, but there are many more friends and family in the square. Many bombard the police who have cordoned off the goods station with questions, but they always receive the same kindly reply: "The train will not arrive until eleven o'clock".

On the platform, helpers have assembled to look after the returning prisoners. Three ambulances stand at the ready. Trucks from all the city districts park beside the tracks to take the returnees and their belongings home. A special train awaits those from the Soviet sector. Twenty-one thermos large pans filled with noodle soup and coffee stand by for those who feel faint. Beside them are huge baskets filled with bread loaves, each weighing 400 grams, provided by Charlottenburg municipal council. Reporters and photographs crowd around the station, and nearby stands a lorry containing the Norddeutscher Rundfunk mobile unit. The Innere Mission and Caritas have sent their volunteer workers.

Most look well, some in better shape than those waiting for them. The joy of reunion at Grunewald station.

Time seems to have stood still. Suddenly, though, excitement begins to run through the crowd of waiting people. It is exactly two thirty. The train enters the station. And at the same time, the sun shines through the clouds, and many women are no longer trembling due to the cold.

In carriage 29, the men drink and laugh. Many are wearing civilian clothes, though most are dressed in worn, faded British uniforms. The train stops, and nearly everyone climbs down from the goods wagon.

Some returning prisoners look neither right nor left at the faces of those seeking their loved ones. They walk firmly ahead, their eyes glazed over, rhythmically striking the ground before them with their sticks. Men for whom no one is waiting.

20 October 1946

The first free elections since 1933

Elections to the municipal assembly take place. The turn-out is exceptional: 93%. The SPD wins 48.7% of the votes, narrowly failing to obtain an absolute majority. The CDU takes second place with 22.5%, followed by the SED with 19.8%. Obstacles had been placed before the SPD during the election campaign, particularly in the eastern sector of the city. The Soviet forces of occupation had attempted to influence the outcome by banning meetings and seizing newspapers printed in West Berlin.

21 October 1946

The Soviets deport qualified German workers

On this day, the Soviets launch a new action in the city: a plan known as Ossawakin, which sows fear and terror throughout the Berlin population. Under it, they prevent economic recovery in the city and in all territories under Soviet occupation by deporting qualified German workers to Russia. More than 10,000 German scientists, engineers, technicians and skilled workers from certain key industries are "transferred". Those affected, forced to sign declarations of consent, must leave their homes with their families by the night of October 22. (They will place their skills and knowledge at the services of the USSR for a period of five years).

The background to this move is provided by the policy of dismantlement that the Soviet Union has been pursuing to date, though with little success. Everything that can be removed from German companies is transported to the Soviet Union. Once there, though, most machinery cannot be used due to the lack of skilled workers. The idea behind Ossawakin is to enable the Soviets to solve this problem.

23-24 November 1946

Six robberies end in murder in 48 hours

The police report does not really cause fear to spread. A stringed instrument maker, Reinhold Reichert is found in the dining room of his house at 44, Beusselstrasse, Berlin NW 87. Lying on the ground, killed by several knife wounds in the chest.

The criminal police are called to the home of Adrian Uschinski, 60 years of age, 41, Holsteinische Strasse, Wilmersdorf. Uschinski and his wife are lying on their bed, stabbed to death. A few days previously, 32-year-old Margot Bold and her 18-

month-old baby are found in bed in their apartment at 36,
Oranienstrasse with their skulls fractured... We do not hear the
police report to the end, but even more murders have been
committed.

(From the time the Berlin crime squad was reformed in May
1945 until 10 February 1946, 142 murders have been committed. All those committed in 1945 except for five have been
cleared up. But this year, the murder rate is going up. The way
these crimes are so quickly cleared up in such complicated circumstances remind some of the spectacularly high success rate
that the Berlin crime squad boasted in the 1920s and 30s,
when no one doubted it is the finest in the world. The success
recorded by the squad during the postwar period can be
explained by the fact that the experts who run formed part of
the force in those earlier days).

16 January 1947

Frozen excrement on the window sill

Berlin is hit by another spell of freezing cold weather. Most
Berliners suffer considerably. Only the war wounded and leg
amputees receive the full coal ration. Do you have to deform
yourself to avoid freezing to death?

It is impossible to use many lavatories situated in the corridors
and stairways of buildings: their doors, toilet seats and window
frames have been taken to use as firewood. Much furniture
has gone the same way. People say that, once it snows,
the temperature will rise. And so they wait, and it snows,
after which the sky becomes bright, shiny blue, but it is even
colder.

Repair teams at the wastewater treatment stations work tireless-
ly. The drainpipes that run from buildings into the sewer system
have frozen. Many pipes no longer work, and nor do many toilets.
The great round sewer system manholes in the streets have
been lifted so that the people can dump their dirty water and faecal matter directly into the collector, but many simply throw it out
of the window.

And necessity proves the mother of invention for many ingenious
Berliners. They wrap their faecal matter in newspaper, leaving
these packages to freeze over night on the window sill or balcony. Next day, on their way to work or the black market, they
discretely throw the parcel onto the ruins that lie all around
them in the city.

Out of the ruins once more

24 June 1947

Ernst Reuter is elected mayor-president.
The Soviets build a wall

In a secret vote, the Greater Berlin city assembly elects Ernst
Reuter as its new mayor-president. At first, however, Reuter is
prevented from taking up his post. The Soviet occupying power
protests against his election because, in their opinion, Reuter is
an anticommunist. Neither the high command nor the Allied Control Council are capable of reaching an agreement. Mayor Louise
Schroeder (SPD) is ordered to take over the post provisionally.

28 October 1947

The Cold War breaks out

The first skirmishes in the coming Cold War take place in Berlin
between the Soviets and the Western Allies. The United States
military governor in Germany, General Lucius D. Clay (who is later
to launch the so-called Luftbrücke, or Airlift, on 24 June 1948)
announces a propaganda offensive by the American forces of
occupation.

General Lucius D. Clay (in
the white coat); right,
Ferdinand Friedensburg;
and behind them, Robert
D. Murphy

The campaign is aimed at making the German population more
familiar with American concepts of democracy. General Clay insists
that there is no longer any reason to temper criticism of communist
policy. The immediate cause of the American offensive is a speech
given on September 20 by the Soviet Military Administration
(SAMAD) head of information services (propaganda) at the second

assembly of the Soviet-backed SED party. In his speech, Colonel
Sergei I. Tulpanov had spoken of the need to free the western sectors from "North American monopoly capitalism". When General
Clay protests against this slander, Marshall Wassili D. Sokolowski,
head of SMAD, retorts that Tulpanov's attacks are totally justified.

2 November 1947

The total of Berliners transferred, detained and disappeared without trace reaches 5,400

Dieter Friede, a journalist on the Berlin newspaper *Der Abend,* is
summoned by telephone to the eastern sector, a meeting from
which he is never to return.
The municipal assembly discusses Friede's disappearance at its
meeting of November 13. Stating that more than 5,400 people
have disappeared from all over Berlin, most without trace, kidnapped or detained mainly for political reasons, Mayor Ferdinand
Friedensburg (CDU) calls on the four Allies to act with regard to
the state of legal insecurity that presently reigns over the city
generally. Next, the city magistrate decides to lodge a complaint
before the Allies.
Investigations into the journalist's whereabouts throw up no clues
at all until June 1 of the following year. On that date, the Soviet-
backed ADN news agency issues a communiqué to the effect that
Friede has been arrested by the Soviet authorities and accused of
spying for the USA and Great Britain. Immediately after this news
goes it, the Soviets deny that there is any truth in the story.

18 March 1948

Ground prepared for the establishment of the GDR

At the Second German People's Congress, also attended by
some delegates from West Berlin, the First German People's
Council (predecessor to the GDR's People's Chamber) elects Wilhelm Pieck, Otto Nuschke and Wilhelm Külz as its presidents.

(On 30 November 1948, during the blockade, the city councillors
from the Soviet sector, meeting in an extraordinary session,
declaring that the Magistrate has been deposed. In his place, they
elect as mayor-president of East Berlin a SED politician and son of
the previous president, Friedrich Ebert, as well as a "provisional
democratic Magistrate" in the Soviet style. The German Democratic Republic (GDR) is officially established on 7 October 1949).

Out of the ruins once more

23 June 1948

Monetary reform deepens the rift between the Allies

On June 22, the Western powers give the Soviets the signal of approval for they monetary reform that they are demanding. In doing so, they declare their willingness to recognise the *Ostmark* (East German Mark) used in the Soviet occupied sector in West Germany, along as the new currency is introduced and administered under joint control. This condition is rejected by the Soviets.

Berliners bid the Reichsmark farewell.

After separate monetary reform in East and West Berlin: money changing in an office in Bahnhof Zoo.

Despite the protests, on June 23, the Soviet Military Administration (SMAD) orders monetary reform to take effect the Soviet Occupation Zone of Germany (SBZ, in its German acronym), including the entire perimeter of Greater Berlin. Just after midnight, the mayor-president of Berlin, Ferdinand Friedensburg, receives the order to immediately put into effect the conversion from the Reichsmark to the "German mark issued by the *Deutschen Notenbank*" throughout the Soviet Occupation Zone in the four sectors of the city.

Nonetheless, at noon next day, the western commanders of the city ban the monetary reform in their sectors. Instead, the following day, they order conversion to the Mark issued by the *Bank Deutscher Länder* (Bank of the German States), introduced throughout the western zones of Germany on June 24. In Berlin's East sector, as in the entire SBZ zone, it is forbidden, on penalty of large fines, to own West German Marks, though the East Mark is recognised in the western sectors along with the so-called "D-Mark" until 20 March 1949.

That same day

Trouble at the Greater Berlin City Hall

On 23 June 1948, a day before the blockade takes effect, unbelievable scenes occur at the City Hall, where Berlin's city councillors are meeting. The City Hall lies in the centre of the Soviet sector, a circumstance the Soviets take advantage of to terrorise Berlin's elected representatives. They load thousands of young people onto trucks, take them to the doors of the City Hall and leave them there to cause trouble.

Many occupy the rooms, block off all exits, force their way into the meeting chamber and threaten the councillors. The police, under the command of the communist president Markgraf, watch the assault, but do not intervene. Those who witnessed these events later recount the story: "When the disturbances began to become really dangerous, a woman took the stand. She looked small, thin and fragile to all there. She had an intelligent face and is wearing rimless glasses that are too big for her. Nothing indicated any nervousness. A vast silence invaded the chamber. This woman was Louise Schroeder, acting mayor of Berlin..."

With the SED votes against, the city councillors decide to dismiss the head of police, Markgraf. In his place, they appoint the social democrat, despite Soviet opposition.

Next, the president of the city council, Otto Suhr, transfers its sessions to the British sector. All SED members remain in the east. This is how the division of Berlin city council begins to take material effect.

Demonstration of SED supporters outside East Berlin City Hall during the assembly devoted to the introduction of the new currency in the western sectors.

Out of the ruins once more

24 June 1948
Surrounded and cut off: the blockade

Early risers hope this new day will be sunny. Little do they suspect that one of the darkest days in the Cold War is about to fall upon them: the total blockade of half the city. At Allied Control Council, at Soviet command and even at the new city assembly, monetary reform has caused violent confrontation. The Soviets cut off all streets, railway lines and canals to the western sectors. This is a complete blockade, by land and water. General Lucius D. Clay calls Washington. Washington needs time to think. Meanwhile, Clay takes a decision under his own responsibility.

At last, the reply from Washington comes: "39 Skymaster transport aircraft have taken off to help supply provisions". Other airplanes will have to be acquired elsewhere. London's response comes more quickly: "100 RAF planes are ready for immediate take off!"

Two hours later, the planes are in the air. Within two days, not just 139 aircraft, but 420 and, very soon, 927 are helping to fly in supplies. One lands every three or four minutes. On July 29, United States General William Turner takes over control of the transport squadrons, organising the operation in painstaking detail. From now on, the "raisin bombers" will land at a suicidal rate of one every 90 seconds. Their buzzing engines are music to Berliners' ears. The operation goes ahead without hitches, and even fog cannot halt the planes, which are guided by radar.

"Raisin bombers" fighting hunger:

The aircraft flies over a group of curious bystanders. Planes land day and night at Tempelhof Airport.

The Airlift saved West Berliners from dying of hunger, but cost the lives of 49 Americans and British.

The aircraft carry food, coke, newspapers, operating tables, copper wire, bales of cloth, wood, steel, in short, anything needed to ensure that Berliners and the Berlin economy are kept alive. It is the Airlift... And Berliners, once more, even during this hardest of tests, continue to be as ingenious as always, as well as not losing their sense of humour, calling the planes come to save them "raisin bombers". Over the eleven months that the blockade lasted, US, British and French pilots bring in nearly 2.5 million products to the city on more than 250,000 flights. However "20 American and 29 British pilots gave their lives so that two million people would not have to sacrifice their freedom or human rights to a dictatorship", as the newspapers said.

The monument to the Airlift at Tempelhof Airport (known by grateful Berliners as the "Hungerharke", or hunger-rake) is a symbol of both thanks and friendship, as the victorious powers showed themselves to be true friends in adversity towards the people of Berlin throughout the crisis.

Berliners call the monument to the Airlift the "Hungerharke" (hunger-rake).

Ernst Reuter unveiled the monument to the Airlift at Tempelhofer Airport on 10 July 1951.

1 July 1948
Four-power administration splits

When the Soviets withdrew from the allied command in Berlin, it spelled the end of the administration of the city by the four powers, escalating the confrontation between the Cold War fronts and making relations even bitterer. From now on, the victorious powers will administer their sectors according to their own ideology. The break-up of Germany is coming ever closer. The idea of dividing Berlin becomes more real. Soviet ambitions to include the western sectors in their area of command become clearer, the mere thought more atrocious.

26 August 1948
Riots shake the city's parliament

This day marks one of the most serious incidents ever to come to pass at the city hall. As usual, the city's parliament is meeting when lorries suddenly disgorge thousands of young trouble-makers, previously fuelled up by Soviet gifts of drink, cigarettes and sausages. They have a job to do, and they duly give it their all. First they shout their protests, then they attack. Heated scenes take place, and fighting ensues, with many arrests made. The non-communist councillors now realise that they cannot carry on meeting in this building in the Soviet sector without running the risk of exposure to ever more brutal attacks.

6 September 1948
City councillors flee to West Berlin

Three mayors around one table (from left to right):

Ernst Reuter,
Otto Suhr,
Louise Schroeder.

Once more, this day, many so-called demonstrators, accompanied by armed members of Markgraf's police, invade the city hall. Security guards, identified by their armbands, are arrested and taken away by Markgraf's men. The session, called for noon, cannot begin. The president of the city council, Otto Suhr, is obliged to transfer this interrupted meeting and all future sessions to Steinplatz in the British sector of West Berlin.
As night falls on this same day, in the absence of SED members, the city assemble agrees to call new elections.
(On 7 December 1948, Ernst Reuter is re-elected as mayor-president).

15 November 1948
HO "Handels-Organisation" free trade shops open

Six days previously, in the *Berliner Zeitung*: "On November 15, the first two free trade shops planned for Berlin by the re-established traders association. The shops are within easy reach in the East Berlin sector. A shop specialising in food products has opened in Neue Königstrasse, whilst the second shop specialises

Out of the ruins once more

in basic goods, domestic appliances and clothing. It will be located at 304, Frankfurter Allee. According to our sources, the prices at these shops may be seven or eight times higher than the pre-war price, reaching black market levels".

At around this time, black market prices are skyrocketing. Flour and pasta sell at 18 DM (Deutschmark, the German Mark) a kilo, a 100 g bar of chocolate sells at between 18 and 20 DM, a bar of soap costs 4-10 DM, silk stockings go for 30 DM the pair, and women's shoes cost between 300 and 400 DM. For pockets not so deep, there is cotton thread at 80 Pfennigs and darning thread at 1.50 DM. A pair of underpants costs at least 25 DM. It's almost better to buy food for the nerves. Cakes can be bought over the counter for 80 Pfennigs each.

Today is opening day, and there are enormous crowds outside the HO shop in Frankfurter Allee. Those first to arrive have been waiting for two hours so as not to be the last, becoming the first of those that can no longer buy anything. Not everyone has come to buy, but all have come to look.

Inside the shop, the lamps shake. *The Eye Witness*, this week's feature film, is on, too. The birth of the HO. Future generations will make their living from this store.

Opening of the first HO shop in 1948.

Peoples of the world, look upon this city!

9 September 1948

Platz der Republik (Republic Square), over which the Reichstag looks out, has never known an atmosphere such as today's. In a passionate appeal, Ernst Reuter, elected mayor-president despite Communist opposition, and officially sworn in on 7 December 1948, calls for help for Berlin under the blockade. "Today is the day when the people of Berlin raise their voice. The people of Berlin today call on the entire world (...) Peoples of the world, you, people in North America, in England, in France, in Italy! Look upon this city and recognise that you may not and cannot abandon these people!"

The background to Reuter's heart-felt appeal are the negotiations that today took place in the Control Council building, where Berlin's fate is at stake. People are afraid that the western Allies will "swap" them with the Soviets, turning them over to Communist rule.

Ernst Reuter's passionate appeal at the largest demonstration since the end of the war, attended by more than 350,000 people.

Peoples of the world, look upon this city!

2 December 1948
Smugglers, black marketeers and opportunists

Salon Daisy, named after the owner of the club, a woman aged little more 50 years old who could easily weigh 200 kilos, stands in a back street off the Kurfürstendamm, which has regained its status as the smartest area in Berlin. Daisy is an experienced woman and allows the curious New York reporters to have a look in her back rooms. "They are all women who give excellent company," she assures the gathering, "Most are married. But they had to come here six months ago. Then there were things going on…"

Friends of the house can, as always, go to an apartment above where a gaming room opened in summer 1945. There is everything – roulette, baccarat, etc – and much luxury. The only thing is, there are not many gamblers. "Before, from autumn 1945 and spring 1948, we used to take a million and a half in every night. What will become of Berlin?"

Previously, the guests were, above all, foreigners, members of the many trade delegations that had become established in Berlin, principally representatives from the Balkan states that collaborated with the Russians, and not always in the most transparent way. Before monetary reform, business was booming. A litre bottle of Slibowitz, which sold in Yugoslavia for 30 dinars and in Berlin might cost 10 marks, went for 280 marks here. The huge profits the business generated enabled her to buy everything she could find: sewing needs, cooking salt, penholders, adding machines…

Street patrols: the police search suspected black marketeers.

Then came monetary reform and the blockade, and the tap was turned off on this great business. At first sight, it seemed that the blockade had suffocated the last chance for doing business in that ruined city of rubble, but the truth was much different. Instead of shortages, what happened was that for some people everything was available once more, but this time on the black market. In July, August, September and October and even now in the harsh midwinter, there is an abundance of goods for sale in West Berlin. Caviar, eggs, eels, fabric, fur coats, gramophones, vehicle tyres, petrol and dollars. It is easy to see that such a large and complicated city as Berlin cannot really be blockaded, at least as far as a determined gang of clever tricksters are concerned.

The blockade is broken, above all, by petty cross-border smuggling, though gunfights sometimes ensue. Nowadays, smugglers concentrate, above all, on taking goods from the west into the east, obtaining profits of a couple of hundred marks every night.

Peoples of the world, look upon this city!

Once over the border, these goods are immediately sent to Berlin, for that is where the prices are highest, by far. Goods also enter blockaded West Berlin from the eastern sector. It is even possible to see hundreds of farmers every day, carrying heavy rucksacks, on local trains, heading for Berlin. These farmers, who live in the Soviet-occupied zone, have their sights firmly set on the Western mark. All of a sudden, those cunning and unscrupulous enough can make a healthy profit from the differences in prices and currencies in the two zones. For that matter, the Airlift is there for something. It is relatively cheap to transport up to one hundred kilos to and from Berlin. In this way, therefore, millions of cigarettes and tonnes of lard, butter and chocolate are flown into the city. In Berlin, these goods sell for two or three times their original purchase price.

But breaking the blockade is not a German monopoly. Many Soviet officials enjoy good enough relations with some border guard commander who will let them take a vehicle out of Berlin. The price per person is 250 Western marks. No documents are needed, and no questions are asked. Members of Czech, Polish and, until recently, Yugoslavian military missions bring huge quantities of North American articles to West Berlin as goods in transit, where they sell them for dollars which can then be changed into Western marks. And all under the protection of diplomatic immunity.

There also exists the American variant of Airlift smuggling. Not all the pilots who fly in day and night turn their noses up at the chance of doing a little business and bringing in a little coffee, a

Illegal east-west trade at Bahnhof Zoo minutes before a raid.

Peoples of the world, look upon this city!

couple of hundred boxes of cigarettes or anything else that comes to hand with them.

The more difficult smuggling becomes during the months the blockade lasts, the more ingenious the tricks that are invented. The Western powers' communication departments are well informed about the most significant of these. Though they do not know the details, much less what goes on before the deals are made, they are perfectly aware, for example, that vehicles are driving around Berlin whose number plates are pure works of engineering. In theory, they belong to Bulgarians, Chinese or South Africans. Some such vehicles, stopped and searched, turn out to have false roofs and floors used to high huge amounts of US dollars and Western marks.

One indispensable condition for any smuggling activity is that the person who carries it out must be able to move around freely. Permits to cross through the different zones and airplane tickets to and from West Berlin are the most sought-after items amongst black marketers. Officially, a return ticket costs around 150 Western marks. A pass from one zone to another is free, the only problem being that, generally speaking, no mortal can obtain one. In summer and autumn 1948, the black market price for a permit and an airplane ticket is around 400 marks. At about this time, though, just before Christmas, this price goes up by 50%, and few doubt that it will continue to rise as long as Berlin is still under blockade.

What these lucrative smuggling operations involving manufactured articles are customers. Berliners are running out of money. An anonymous army of poor people are turning to contraband. Each smuggles for himself, using enormous creative abilities to keep his fire burning.

"The sharpness of replies by all Berliners who have not been asked".

"The Insulaner... does not lose his calm, the Insulaner does not stand on ceremony, the Insulaner imperturbably awaits the day when his island will once more form part of a beautiful terra firme".

28 December 1948

The best programme for perseverance in Berlin

They sing freely to themselves, the people of Berlin, on the RiaS radio station, the *Voice of the Free World*, set up by the Americans in 1946 as a way of countering the propaganda machine controlled by the Soviets (Berliner Rundfunk radio).

For the first time this Christmas, the people of Berlin joyfully hear for the first time the chorus to the unmistakable song that *Günther Neumann and His "Insulaners"* will make famous every week as part of the cabaret programme they will broadcast on the radio every week.

Peoples of the world, look upon this city!

Günter Neumann during rehearsals for his cabaret show, broadcast on RiaS.

The company of "*Insulaners*", which includes Günther Neumann and his wife Tatjana Sais as well as other popular cabaret artistes such as Walter Groß and Agnes Windeck, has made a fantastic contribution to restoring Berlin's fame as Germany's leading cabaret since Hitler first took power.

That these "*Insulaners*" should begin to cheer up the people of Berlin during the blockade imposed on them is, of course, no coincidence. The city is reacting to the conditions to which they are subjected by outside powers with all the means available. Because the worst could happen any day, at every hour there is the possibility that the Russians will fall on West Berlin. And this anxious awaiting the world is the daily nightmare that faces most West Berliners.
But amongst all the unanswered question, one in particular, as to how long the Airlift can keep feeding the millions of people in the western sectors, how long the western Allies will retain the patience to continue supporting the financial and organisational burden involved, this is the conundrum that most concerns Berliners over the course of all these hours, days and weeks.

The SED labels the RiaS cabaret artistes "dangerous warmongers". Party officials are furious, but they are powerless against the satirical humour launched against them. No eastern remedy is known to ward off these puns, this mordant irony, this subtle satire, which hides much deeper meaning. In his report from Berlin, the young Reich capital, 1877-1883, the Danish literary critic Georg Brandes wrote the following: "The Berlin *tone* is considered in Germany as a whole, and not just in the city itself, as extremely critical. And critical in a particularly negative sense, careless to the point of shamelessness and full of caustic humour. (...) The Spree will cease to flow before a true Berliner fails to provide a sharp answer to a question".

Peoples of the world, look upon this city!

11 February 1949
Suicide rates rising in Berlin

A woman dead in the Landwehrkanal. Suicide?

At 8.30 am, Gertrud K., 20 years of age, from Friedenau, throws herself off the train just as it is entering Wilmersdorf station, dying instantly. However, the young woman is about give birth to a child, and her death gives life to her son. The newborn baby is quickly taken to Gertrauden Hospital, dying three hours later. Berlin is scandalised, but only up to a certain point. Throughout the day, the police report on several more suicides in all four sectors. This month, 127 people have taken their own lives. Most of them are old people who can no longer face the day to day problems. Or whose eyes have seen too much horror... and all they want to do is close them.

12 May 1949
The blockade ends

At last! Berlin breathes again! At 1 am, convoys of vehicles begin moving through the Dreilinden and Helmstedt checkpoints, both towards West Germany and also in the opposite direction, towards West Berlin. The blockade, which has lasted nearly eleven months, ends with the entry into force of an agreement between the western powers and the Soviet Union, negotiated between the US and USSR delegates to the United Nations Security Council. Previously, the Soviet Union had given up its intention of introducing the Eastern mark in West Berlin. Although it is now possible once more to reach Berlin by road, the Airlift continues until October 6. Nonetheless, West Berliners will have to get by without many things they might have had were it not for the blockade. Each home receives just 25 pounds of coal to last the whole winter, and the population lives, basically, on dried foods. There is electrical power for just four hours a day. Looking back, US historians have praised the self-discipline the besieged population demonstrated: "One of the aspects of the crisis that most draws our attention is the behaviour of West Berlin's civil population during the blockade. (…) Although they knew that their city might be overrun at any time by Russian troops, Berlin's people stood firm in their resistance to Soviet threats and promises. They learned to live in danger, even with a certain degree of ease." The outstanding conduct of those encircled by the Soviets is also attributed to a large extent to the enormous influence of the city's mayor-president, Ernst Reuter, whose down-to-earth speeches expressed the people's feelings and what could help them to carry on. Along with Willy Brandt, Reuter (who died in Berlin on 29 September 1953) continues even today to be considered by most older Berliners as the best-loved mayor of the city since the Second World War.

26 May 1949:

The German Federal Republic is founded. The seat of government is established in Bonn, a small town on the banks of the River Rhine.

7 October 1949
The GDR is established

The Second German People's Council, elected by the Third German People's Congress, meets in Berlin. After discussing the political situation, the Council proclaims itself a "provisional people's chamber empowered by the constitution of the German Democratic Republic agreed on 19 March 1949 and approved on May 30 by the Third German People's Congress". The news causes considerable commotion in West Berlin. The next day, thousands of Berliners, along with the city councillors, demonstrate before Schöneberger City Hall, the office of the mayor-president, Ernst Reuter, against the establishment of a separate state in the eastern part of the country.

Generalissimus
Josef W. Stalin

In May 1945, the occupying Soviet power celebrates victory over Hitler's Germany in the eastern sector, installing huge posters of Stalin.

21 December 1949
East Berlin's Prachtstraße renamed Stalinallee

By order of the magistrate of East Berlin, Frankfurter Allee, the impressive, wide avenue linking the Mitte, Friedrichshain and Lichtenberg districts, is now renamed after the Soviet leader Josef Stalin, a mass murderer who will eventually be recognised as such even by the communists.

Peoples of the world, look upon this city!

Stalinallee.

The name change is timed to coincide with a huge demonstration in East Berlin, when the first stone in a housing reconstruction programme is laid in what was formerly known as Frankfurter Allee (thereafter, Stalinallee becomes a repository of typical Socialist architecture. In 1961, during the de-Stalinisation campaign, part of this impressive avenue is renamed Karl-Marx-Allee, whilst the other part is restored to its original title: Frankfurter Allee).

Life and suffering in East Berlin

11 January 1950

Brecht stages *Mother Courage*

The decision to stage this theatrical work may turn out to be prophetic: directed by Bert Brecht and Erich Engel, East Berlin's Deutsches Theater presents Brecht's play *Mother Courage and Her Children*. In it, Brecht seeks to portray both conflictive social situations and contradictory human behaviour. The German playwright amply achieves this objective in his character, Mother Courage. Despite having a warm human nature, Mother Courage is nevertheless firm in her avarice, behaving with considerable cunning, limited only by her lack of intelligence, whenever she has to think beyond her daily bread.

The play, written in 1939, tells the story of Mother Courage, a canteen woman, during the Thirty Years' War. Over the course of the play, she loses her three children, her belongings and her friends. At the end, she harnesses herself to an empty wagon and pulls it off towards an empty horizon.

The production, the first by Helene Weigel and Brecht's own theatre company, the Berliner Ensemble, becomes a hit worldwide. The GDR regime reaps undeserved fruit from this resounding success, as its political leaders appropriate Brecht (who was to die in Berlin on August 14), manipulating him to their own ends.

Actress and theatre director Helene Weigel in her role as *Mother Courage*.

29 February 1950

The GDR's economy plunges into depression

It becomes clear that the East Berlin economy will not meet the targets set. This is due to several reasons: war damage, the forced deportation of qualified workforce and the reparations imposed by the Soviets, which must be paid to the USSR. The essence of economic development is rapid consolidation of the state sector.

(Since the foundation of East Berlin, from early-1949 to late 1950, gross production of State enterprise – VEB, or people-owned enterprise, in its German abbreviation, increases from 47% to 75%. Some 51% of the retail trade and agriculture are still in private hands, but the nationalisation process ploughs on).

Life and suffering in East Berlin

8 April 1950
Berlin's Al Capone sentenced to death

He is the most famous Berlin post-war gangster. A Berlin court condemns 18-year-old gang leader Werner Gladow to death for murder and grievous bodily harm, with eleven robberies taken into account.

Between 1948 and 1949, Gladow and his accomplices, two of whom receive the same sentence, had perpetrated many robberies, never hesitating to use firearms. Gladow was finally arrested in East Berlin on 3 June 1949 after a spectacular gunfight.

(Later, his story will be turned into a film).

27 May 1950
First meeting of FDJ dinosaurs

The meeting organised by the Free German Youth movement (Freie Deutsche Jugend, or FDJ, in German) begins. This huge event, lasting until May 30, is attended by some 700,000 young people, 30,000 of them from the Federal German Republic, as well as many foreign delegates.

The meeting takes place amid grave attacks by the GDR on the federal government in Bonn. The culminating point is an 8-hour march by more than half a million people, who parade past the tribune erected for dignitaries near Lustgarten Park.

Despite the strict border controls between the sectors, around 30,000 FDJ members take the chance to visit West Berlin.

The East marches against the West: Demonstration incentral Berlin.

In response to a call by mayor-president Ernst Reuter, an advisory campaign is launched to provide young people above all with the possibility of debating and receiving political information.

During preparations for the "German meeting", great alarm was caused by the FDJ announcement that hundreds of thousands would march on West Berlin. As a result, the occupying powers and the local authorities in the Western sectors are forced to adopt tight security measures. Although the FDJ eventually gives up this plan, the "German meeting" in the Western sector is awaited with enormous concern.

16 October 1950
Growing waves of refugees

Refugees from the Eastern zone on their way to the camp in West Berlin.

The growing waves of refugees cause serious problems to the West Berlin magistrate due to lack of accommodation for them. All the camps are full, and new provisional camps are constantly needed. With 300,000 unemployed people in West Berlin already, it is extremely difficult to bear additional economic burdens. This year, 124.9 million marks are provided to give aid to refugees and war victims. The magistrate calls on the Red Cross for assistance, and on the social welfare association for workers.

Panic takes hold of many East Germans when the GDR is about to be absorbed by the Soviet Bloc. This year, a total of 197,788 people from the GDR flee from communist government, with young people under 25 years making up half of all these refugees. It is estimated that West Berlin takes in more than 80,000 people who have left the eastern sectors due to political or economic reasons.

GDR leaders observe this phenomenon with growing concern. In 1949, following the founding of the GDR, 59,245 citizens left the country. The following year, estimates not made public point to further increases in this flow of refugees (the estimated figure for 1951 is 165,640 refugees). Secret studies warn the GDR leadership of the threat of slow social breakdown. Danger lies, too, in the fact that more and more skilled workers, scientists and artists are leaving the country to seek better living and working conditions in the West.

24 October 1950
The bell of freedom rings out in the West

...after his six-week "crusade" around America.

The GDR regime observes events in the Western sector with a scornful smile. At a ceremony which takes place outside Schöneberg City Hall, the American military governor in Germany, General Lucius D. Clay, gives Berlin the liberty bell cast in England, a copy of the North American liberty bell.
Before being brought to Berlin on October 22, the bell was taken around the United States in a "crusade for freedom" launched by Clay. The bell was paid for by donations made by 16 million Americans, whose signatures are now kept in the Town Hall, expressing their desire that Berlin's people will one day find freedom.

6 November 1950
The GDR regime demolishes the Royal Palace

Ignoring all protests, even those from amongst their own people, leaders of the GDR regime do away with practically all reminders of Berlin's singular, eventful and adventurous history. Since September, constant explosions denote the demolition of the Royal Palace and with it the rupture with Berlin's Prussian traditions.

The square before the Royal Palace, before and after demolition.

The Royal Palace could have been rebuilt.

The damaged building, ancient residence of the House of Hohenzoller and the most outstanding monument in central Berlin (Unter den Linden), must now give way to the parade ground planned for construction on the site. In May 1951 it is decided to build a provisional stand here, to be joined to a square that can accommodate crowds of up to 350,000 people.
The decision is agreed by the GDR Council of Ministers on August 23. Countless personalities from both East and West had urged that the Royal Palace should be rebuilt, as the damage could have been repaired.

5 August 1951

Two million people attend the World Festival

The GDR seeks to impress the West with a colossal propaganda exercise. The Third World Festival of Youth and Students begins, attended, according to official figures, by two million young people from both East and West Germany and 26,000 delegates from 104 countries.

Nearly half the participants secretly visit West Berlin.

At the service of the communist peace propaganda machine, the festival will run until August 19, featuring sporting and cultural events and, above all, political meetings. On August 15, some 10,000 FDJ members distribute flyers in Neukölln, Wedding and Kreuzberg, student and working-class districts in West Berlin.

Under the excuse of maintaining peace and order, the West Berlin police use water cannons and batons against this crowd, and 115 FDJ demonstrators are arrested. In East Berlin, the organisers cannot prevent hundreds of thousands from amongst those attending the World Festival from visiting West Berlin.

26 May 1952

The GDR establishes the first blockades

The GDR Council of Ministers announces that it is closing the border with the Federal Republic. Although the checkpoints between East and West Berlin and remain open, the east regime implements a series of measures against the West in and around the city.

And so it is that, just a day later, telephone connections between the two halves of the city are cut off. The next day, most road links between West Berlin and surrounding areas are cordoned off by primitive embankments and barriers made from tree trunks. Only access roads between West Berlin and federal territory are left open. At the same time, the GDR forbids West Berliners from entering the East.

On May 31, the People's Police, along with Soviet troops, occupy key points in West Berlin. The people living there are ordered to abandon their houses before midnight. The three Western powers protest against this blockade and against the suspension of telephone lines.

The GDR rigorously rejects these protests, justifying their actions in cordoning off the city with reference to the Treaty of Germany, signed by the Federal Republic on May 26-27, and the planned European Defence Community, which would lead to the restoration of much of its sovereign rights to West Germany, as well as a contingent of German troops forming part of a multi-national European army.

27 November 1952

West Berliners can no longer shop in East Berlin

The magistrate of East Berlin orders that from now on food and industrial products shall only be given to those who have the corresponding rationing card, accompanied by their identity card. This effectively prevents West Berliners from purchasing anything in the eastern sector of the city, unless they work there.

Through this measure, the GDR purports to combat the "unchecked purchasing" of "cheating, speculating" West Berliners. The reality is that, every day, thousands of West Berliners can buy food, shoes and even bread for their own families and for their friends using eastern money that costs only one-fifth of their own currency at exchange bureaux near the border in West Berlin. They use their money to buy all the food they can find, leaving East Berliners wide-eyed before empty shelves.

On the "small scale", currency auctions are also lucrative for some East Berliners. Some of them, mostly young men, return empty beer bottles to Western shops. Then they exchange their Western Pfennigs (three per bottle) into Eastern

...it costs them little to empty East Berlin shop shelves.

marks and, the next day, back home, they can buy five times more beer or give their girlfriends a nice present.

Another reason behind the ban on Westerners shopping in the east is that the GDR is faced by food shortages that threaten to spread since, due to farm collectivisation, more and more farmers are fleeing with their families to the West. The figures speak for themselves: more than 51,000 in 1952 and 1953 alone.

Board showing the East Mark trading price at an exchange bureau in Kurfürstendamm during the early-1950s.

Before this crisis began the East Berlin magistrate had encouraged West Berliners to purchase products in his part of the city. For example, by bringing down food and drink prices, causing trade problems with West Berlin. West Berliners found the exchange rates offered at the many bureaux de change in their city particularly attractive, yet another reason to shop in East Berlin (in November 1952, 100 Eastern marks cost just 22.10 DM). All social classes take advantage of this chance to shop at extraordinarily low prices.

16 June 1953
East Berlin workers strike

The first workers to go on strike are those engaged in the works on Stalinallee. The reason is the 10% increase in the production target which entered into effect on June 1 and entailed a large decrease in wages. In protest, work stoppages had already taken place at points all over East Berlin. On June 16, *Tribüne*, the GDR's trade union newspaper, publishes an article defending the increase, and the workers strike once more.

Nine o'clock in the morning: some 300 workers form a timid demonstration and march on the building occupied by the union to deliver a written protest. On the way, the crowd grows and the People's Police let them through. The demonstrators find union headquarters closed, so they make for the ministry buildings in Leipziger Straße. They now number more than 10,000. The crowd demands talks with SED general secretary Walter Ulbricht and GDR prime minister Otto Grotewohl. However, the pair refuse to meet demonstrators.

At around 2 pm, the minister for mining, iron and steel address-es the crowd, informing the striking demonstrators that the SED has taken an urgent decision: the increased production targets are to be withdrawn with immediate effect. The demonstrators do not allow the minister to finish his speech. Now they demand the government's resignation and call a general strike for the fol-lowing day.

The workers demand the resignation of the entire government.

Demonstrators outside the former Reich Air Ministry in Leipziger Straße.

Returning along Stalinallee to Alexanderplatz, the seething crowd commandeers a SED vehicle mounted with loudspeakers and uses it to propagate its own slogans. At around 5 pm, the demonstration breaks up, and discussion groups are set up all over East Berlin. Agitators and SED workers are expelled from these.

The report on the demonstration broadcast by the RiaS is instru-mental in informing about the striking workers' demands on the afternoon of June 16, and the story spreads like wildfire through-out East Berlin and the entire GDR.

Life and suffering in East Berlin

17 June 1953

The popular uprising...

Friedrichstraße, near the
sector border.

7 am – 1 pm

In East Berlin and many GDR cities, more than 300,000 workers from the nationalised companies go on strike. Demonstrations and disturbances take place throughout the day, become
ever more violent and finally taking the shape of a popular uprising. East Berlin, along with the industrial regions of Central Germany, is the focal point in this revolt. Work stops at practically
all factories, and nearly all the machinery is stopped. At around
7 pm, 20,000 striking building workers gather in Straußberger
Platz. At the same time, workers from many industrial enterpris-
es head for the city centre; 12,000 employees from the Hen-
nigsdorf iron and steel works and 16,000 from
Reichsbahnbauunion de Velten cross the French sector of the
city (Wedding-Reinickendorf). Meanwhile, SED posters are ripped
from walls in the eastern part of the city. Newsstands go up in
flames. The first confrontations with the People's Police occur
outside the ministry buildings.

Life and suffering in East Berlin

Between 10 and 11 am, East Berlin transport companies suspend services. Most employees have joined the uprising. The strikers the previous day, with their limited demands, have now lost control of events. The revolt threatens to turn into a revolution. Soviet tanks thunder down Unter den Linden, taking Friedrichstraße to Checkpoint Charlie before quickly turning into Potsdamer Platz. Dozens advance towards the Ulbrichtstadion border checkpoint, through the Brandenburg Gate and into Potsdamer Platz towards the Oberbaumbrücke bridge in Friedrichshain.

At around 9 am, the first Soviet troops enter East Berlin, taking up positions in the city centre at around noon. The Russian soldiers do not open fire until protesters tear down the red flag from the Brandenburg Gate.

1 pm – 7 pm

At 1 pm, the Soviet commander-in-chief, Pawel T. Dibrowa, announces that a state of exception has been imposed in East Berlin. Meetings of more than three people are forbidden. Shots are heard all over the city. The situation does not calm down until early afternoon. An evening curfew is also imposed, but the disturbances continue. Several buildings go up in flames. The Soviets do not take control of the situation until around 7 pm. All borders with the Western sectors are closed.

The Oberbaumbrücke bridge in Friedrichshain.

Soviet tanks push their way through the crowd in Friedrichstraße.

Life and suffering in East Berlin

The uprising has failed. That same evening, the Soviet commander-in-chief announces that a Soviet court martial orders the death by firing squad of the West Berliner Willi Göttling, who allegedly took part in the riots. Over the next few days, normal life and suffering resumes in the East once more.

The disturbances cost the lives of 267 workers and 116 SED officials. A further 92 are executed under martial law and many more are sentenced to death. But where were the people in this uprising, which we can practically consider to have been a popular revolt? Many wonder whether the non-violent presence of family and friends of the rebellious workers might have changed the course of events as, disappointed, they return once more to what seems to be their inevitable fate.

(A demonstration outside Schöneberg Town Hall in West Berlin takes place on June 23 to express popular sympathy for the victims of the uprising. A crowd of some 125,000 Berliners assembles before the coffins of seven people who died in these tragic events. Ernst Reuter and Jacob Kaiser address the demonstration, as does Federal Chancellor Konrad Adenauer. June 17 is declared a holiday throughout Federal territory and in West Berlin).

223 shot and beaten to death, and 1,200 sentenced to a total of 6,000 years in prison.

People trying to flee to the West are shot at from Potsdamer Platz.

1953

21 June 1953

GDR government makes mass arrests

Taking up a position for the first time about the June 17 events, the SED describes the uprising as a "fascist provocation" organised from West Germany and Berlin. The GDR government uses the June 17 events as a welcome if forced opportunity to "clean up". The government decides to take action, not only against the spokespeople for the uprising, but also against all those dissidents that have caused so much discomfort. From June 18 on, thousands of alleged "ring-leaders" and "agents provocateurs" are arrested. Soviet military justice and GDR courts condemn at least 22 people to death, whilst a further 1,200 prison sentences totalling 6,000 years are also passed down. Top SED officials are also prosecuted: the justice minister is arrested and the ministry for security is sacked.

25 June 1953

The uprising; practically civil war
Left in the lurch by the West?

The same question is asked again and again all over Berlin. However, the part played by the West in the June 17 events was not so simple as to be reduced to a single question. The allied Western powers played a dramatic, even highly problematic role in what happened that day. What politicians in West Berlin and Germany as a whole revealed more than anything was their powerlessness to do anything.

Both the federal government and the Western powers were taken surprise by the events. More than anything, though, they were overwhelmed by them. They were quickly forced to admit that directly supporting the striking workers over the border post or sending in the Allied army might have led to confrontation with the Soviet forces of occupation, whose back was up against the wall and would have had no other option but to counterattack without warning, sending in its troops and tank units, very superior in number to Western allied forces in Berlin. That would have meant allowing West Berlin to fall into Soviet hands, and the Western powers, which would have been allowed to withdraw peacefully, could hardly have been expected to start a third world war, as they would have found themselves up against not only the Soviets, but all the members of the Warsaw Pact. Europe would have engulfed in flames. This is a scenario which seems more likely than ever to come about in these times of popular uprising.

The Stasi's infamous Hohenschönhausen prison, a place of humiliation and torture for thousands.

(The Western allies' decision not to get involved is hotly debated and criticised by many disappointed victims of the events in East Berlin. However, seen more objectively, with the passing of time, one is forced to conclude that this was the only decision possible).

17 July 1953
The West donates food aid

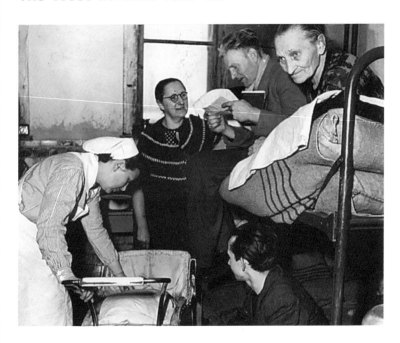

20 September 1956

Members of a family in emergency accommodation. In order to cope with the wave of refugees from the east, emergency shelter was provided at the radio station pavilions.

The mayor of Berlin, Ernst Reuter, announces in a radio interview that West Berlin will donate free food to the population on the other side of the city and in the GDR. Each GDR citizen will receive a parcel to the value of five marks every month. This gesture, apart from helping to alleviate need, also seeks to express the solidarity that all Germans feel with regard to the suppression of the June 17 uprising. Firstly, the Berlin senate and the federal government prepare a million aid parcels, which are handed over by Berlin municipal councils. On the first day alone, more than 100,000 people come from East Germany to collect their parcels. The following day, a further 140,000 flock to the delivery points.
On August 1, Ernst Reuter personally hands over parcel number one million. Meanwhile, a counter-campaign has been launched in the GDR. On August 2, entry into West Berlin is forbidden by decree. At border checkpoints, the People's

Police, known as *Vopos*, seize parcels from people returning home. Even so, hundreds of thousands continue on the following days to enter West Berlin and sign up for the aid parcels at the delivery points. Soon, staff employed to distribute the parcels are overwhelmed, and their number has to be increased to 2,000. On August 3, the senate and the federal government decide to provide a further one and a half million parcels. Provisions also begin to arrive from the United States. This aid campaign has to be halted on August 16 as provisions have run out, and continuing would cause a dangerous shortage of reserve food supplies in West Berlin, since the threat of a second Soviet blockade cannot be ruled out. Up to August 28, more than 2.8 parcels have been distributed, reaching 90% of East Berlin's population.

22 April 1956

300-metre long spy tunnel found

The Soviet military discovers a spy tunnel for those seeking to flee East Berlin in the Treptow district. It begins in Rudow in West Berlin and passes under the border between the sectors, leading some 300 metres into the eastern sector. In the gallery in the east, equipment is found that enabled spies to listen into the Soviet military and GDR telephone communication systems.

The next day, April 23, the Soviet commander-in-chief calls a press conference to announce the discovery, attacking Western secret services for their "murderous attempt at espionage".

West Berlin security police guard the exit.

Life and suffering in East Berlin

14 August 1956

Berlin mourns the great B. B.

Bert Brecht shortly before his death.

Playwright and theatre director Bertolt Brecht dies at his Chausseestraße home in East Berlin at the age of 56 years. Brecht, son of a factory manager, grew up in Augsburg and began to study medicine in Munich until, in 1922, he published his first play, *Baal*. That same year, he received the Kleist Prize for *Drums in the Night*.

In 1924, he moved to Berlin to work as a playwright with the Max Reinhardt theatre company at the Deutsches Theater. In 1926, he began to study the Marxist teachings that would impregnate his future works. His greatest success came with the *Threepenny Opera*. In 1933, Brecht was forced to leave Germany and in 1941, having passed through several European countries, he travelled to the United States. Brecht produced many of his most famous works in exile (for example, *Mother Courage* and *The Caucasian Chalk Circle*). In 1947, he left the United States, firstly living in Switzerland. In 1948, he purchased his last home, this time in East Berlin. Here, with his wife, the great actress Helene Weigel, he founded the Berliner Ensemble, which first performed at its permanent home at the Theater am Schiffbauerdamm on 19 March 1954, its productions going on to achieve worldwide fame.

20 September 1956

GDR refugee number one million

Early today, asylum seeker number one million reached the federal refugee camp in Marienfelde. Parliamentary president Willy Brandt gives out the news in West Berlin at the opening of the 42nd ordinary session of Berlin's chamber of representatives. Brandt reminds the assembly of the tragedy behind this growing wave of refugees. The fact that people are being forced to flee from their own country leads him once more to appeal to state leaders and people to finally give the German people the peace that will again join what should never have been ripped asunder.

27 November 1958

Khrushchev's ultimatum threatens Berlin once more

There is no peace for Berlin. This greatly misused city cannot even pause for breath. In identical notes to the three Western powers, the Federal Republic and the GDR, the Soviet government denies the status of the four powers in Berlin, proposing, moreover, to turn West Berlin into a "free, demilitarised city". The Soviets give a space of six months in which to begin negotiations and, as a precautionary measure, also inform that, should no mutually-agreed solution be found, then all rights governing control of access to West Berlin will be handed over to the GDR. And so begins the second Berlin crisis since the blockade in 1948. In sparking off this emergency, Nikita Khrushchev, the head of the Soviet government, is mounting a frontal attack against the presence in West Berlin of the three Western protecting powers, who are thrown into doubt and confusion by the Soviet demands. Even more concerned are the Berliners themselves since, if Khrushchev withdraws his ultimatum, it will mean that the Western powers have signalled their willingness to negotiate over the Berlin question.

Nikita Khrushchev:
The Western Allies must leave!

27 May 1959
The ultimatum expires. The crisis worsens

This is the day that the ultimatum issued by the Soviet government on November 27 runs out. Reconciliation seems distant, though the Soviets do not look so willing to put their threats into effect. On January 24, during a visit to the United States, the delegate from the Soviet foreign ministry implies that the USSR is not so firmly committed to ensuring that their demand for demilitarisation in West Berlin is satisfied.
(However, on 11 June 1959, the Soviet Union returns to its hard line at the conference of foreign ministers in Geneva. The crisis continues).

7 September 1960
Wilhelm Pieck dies

Wilhelm Pieck, first GDR president after its establishment in 1949, dies at the age of 84 years at his administrative headquarters in Niederschönhausen Castle in Pankow. After completing his apprenticeship as a cabinet-maker, Pieck joined the German Social-Democrat Party (SPD) in 1895. At the end of the First World War in 1918 he shifted his allegiances to the German Communist Party (KPD), and was elected to parliament for the KPD in 1926. In 1933, he emigrated, firstly to France and later to the Soviet Union. He returned to Germany in 1945 and took over leadership of the SED with Otto Grotewohl the following year. In 1949, he was elected president of the GDR. The death of Wilhelm Pieck, an important chapter in the establishment of East Berlin, which many still consider a promising start, will have a desperately disappointing ending for citizens of the GDR, particularly those living in East Berlin.

Life and suffering in East Berlin

For many GDR citizens, Wilhelm Pieck, a warm person, richly appreciated right up until his death, personified a socialism that deserved a chance as it was in the process of maturing and merited the greatest effort.

(On September 10, thousands of East Berliners accompany Wilhelm Pieck on his last journey, from Marx-Engels-Platz to the Baumschulenweg crematorium, where his mortal remains are incinerated. Soon after, Walter Ulbricht establishes the State Council with himself as its all-powerful chairman).

The very image...

10 January 1961
199,188 people flee the East in 1960

Since 1949, more than two and a half million GDR citizens have turned their backs on their own country for different reasons. But in the last three or four years, refugees have simply tired of waiting for things to get better. The GDR regime supports the rumour that many refugees fleeing to the Federal Republic have a bad time of it. However, East Berliners able to see conditions in West Berlin for themselves no longer even bother to laugh at this. The SED-controlled press writes that many refugees have repented and returned. No one believes the figures that are published, because no one knows anyone from amongst those supposed to have come back. It is also said that the Nazis are in control in the West once more. Perhaps it does not matter whether anyone believes this or not. Not even a new Hitler in the West would persuade anyone that life is better in the East. They have always been convinced that nowhere can be as ghastly as the GDR.

15 June 1961
Division date announced

What happens on the borders between the Berlin sectors on the night of August 13 does not come as such a surprise to the Western powers as it will later appear. At a meeting in Vienna, Khrushchev had made it clear to John F. Kennedy that, as occupying powers, the Americans, the British and the French no longer had any rights over Berlin. At a press conference a few days after this conference, Kruschev denies that the Soviets are trying to build a wall in Berlin: "I know of no such intention!" he exclaims, repeating this denial on the radio on 15 June 1961.

That same day, Walter Ulbricht repeats the same lie when asked at a press conference whether the creation of a "Berlin as a free city" means that the border will be established at the Brandenburg Gate in future. The question has nothing to do with walls. However, Ulbricht replies as follows: "I understand by your question that there are in West Germany men who wish that we [would] mobilise the construction workers of the GDR in order to build a wall. I don't know of any such intention. The construction workers of our country are principally occupied with home building... Nobody has the intention of building a wall."

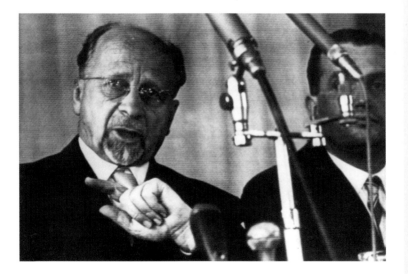

Walter Ulbricht, chairman of the GDR State Council at the international press conference at the East Berlin ministry building during which he made the famous exclamation "Nobody has the intention of building a wall!"

That Kruschev should speak of a "wall" and that, at the same time, apparently by pre-agreement Ulbricht should do the same considerably increased concern amongst people living in the Soviet-occupied zone. The GDR regime never tires of blaming on "Western agents" everything that happens in the Soviet area of occupation.

First call from the new state of madness:

Children in a Red Army paramilitary group playing war games in the Seelow Hills. In the foreground, a boy wearing the helmet of the National People's Army (NVA, from the German Nationale Volksarmee) and carrying a Kalashnikov.

(Later on, the statistics will also disprove those who claimed that the only ones fleeing from the East were those for whom things were not going so well, due to their own fault, needless to say). It is precisely those who are granted favour, such as engineers, technicians, doctors, even police officers and soldiers from the People's Army, that make up the largest percentage of those fleeing. Behind closed doors, Walter Ulbricht declares himself in favour of taking direct action against West Berlin. He is keen to enter the Western sectors, but the Soviet Union refuses to support Ulbricht's plans. Instead, the USSR observes its interests, precisely drawn out, and limits its attacks to its former occupied zone, in East Berlin and the GDR, to resolve the refugee problem.

Building a wall continues to be one of the possibilities the Soviets are toying with, and there is no doubt that Khrushchev agreed the plan with Ulbricht after their meetings at the Vienna summit, when he was convinced that the Western powers, at heart, would go along with such a plan, since such a wall would also help them to protect their own sectors. And so it is that the way opens up to building the wall. Ulbricht has approval to go ahead with the plan.

Early-August 1961
The suspense becomes unbearable

Over the first days of August, East Berliners' nervous systems are subjected to the most dreadful test. Many can sense it. There is something in the air, a terrible danger is bearing down on them. And many who feel nothing are caught up in the mood anyway. But none of them knows what is going to happen on August 13, not even the most pessimistic predictions could foresee such a thing ...

...But before going on, let us take another look at lifestyles in West Berlin over the last ten years.

Go West. Life on the "island"

6 June 1951

21 nations take part in the first Berlin International Film Festival

The first Berlin International Film Festival opens at the Titania-Palast in Steglitz, with the participation of 21 nations entering 34 feature films and around 100 documentaries. Three years after the blockade, the Americans establish this festival, known to Berliners as the Berlinale, to provide a "showcase for the West in the *Red Sea*".
At the end of this first festival, an international jury awards gold, silver and bronze "bears" in eight film categories.
(For the first ten years, until 1961, it is stars from Hollywood above all who give the festival its glamour, again and again tarnished by the crises that hit Berlin. The workers' uprising of 17 June 1953, for example, will cause many superstars to cancel their participation).

Boulevard Berlin
The showcase for the West in the "Red Sea".

Berliners in the thralls by Hollywood fever at the Film Festival on Kurfürstendamm.

Go West. Life on the "island"

11 July 1951
"We are brothers. Do not forget"
300,000 attend the Kirchentag

The closing ceremony at the packed Olympic Stadium.

The third "Kirchentag" (church gathering) opens at the Marienkirche church in East Berlin, in the Neuer Markt, under the slogan "We are brothers. Do not forget", bringing together Christians from all Germany in both sides of the city.
The opening ceremony is also attended by the GDR president, Wilhelm Pieck, and by the mayor-president of East Berlin, Friedrich Ebert. Some 300,000 people attend the many events programmed. The venues, at the radio tower pavilions and the Werner-Seelenbinder Hall in East Berlin, become so crowded that it quickly becomes necessary to organise parallel events.

23 January 1952
Berlin, city of the press, flourishes once more

The North American High Commissioner for Berlin returns the Tempelhof press to the firm of ULLSTEIN AG. Until 1933, Ullstein was one of the most important newspaper publishers in Germany. Its publications included the *Vossische Zeitung*, the *Berlin-*

er *Illustrierte Zeitung* and the *Berliner Morgenpost*. The National Socialist German Workers Party forced Ullstein to sell the publishing company, which the Nazi Party took over in 1937.
[On 26 September 1952, Ullstein begins printing the *Berliner Morgenpost* once more, its publication having been suspended on 23 April 1945. For the first seven years after the end of the war, the Berlin press enjoys a spectacular boom, and by the end of 1947 a score of newspapers are printed in the city every day).

25 December 1952
Television comes to Berlin

Recording a programme at the studio.

The first television programme, broadcast on the first day of the Christmas holidays, is a documentary about how the song Silent Night was composed.
On December 21, the television studio in East Berlin begins broadcasting a daily two-hour programme. Nordwestdeutsche Rundfunk (NWDR) is the first Western television channel to air a regular series of programmes. Until the end of the year, prerecorded programmes are broadcast from 8 to 10 pm from Berlin, Cologne and Hamburg. The NWDR Tempelhof studios had been transmitting programmes by cable to a broadcasting tower in Berlin-Nikolassee and to the Hamburg studios by frequency modulation since September. On New Year's Day 1953, a network of broadcasting stations is launched that make it possible to broadcast a single signal to the entire Federal Republic.

Leaders of Berlin's Jewish community (from left to right): Heinz Galinski and Leo Witkowski.

28 August 1953
The first Jewish synagogue is established

The reconstruction of Berlin includes the establishment of synagogues in both sides of the city to serve the religious needs of the local Jewish community.

In Rykestraße, a street in East Berlin's Prenzlauer Berg district, a ceremony takes place to reopen the biggest synagogue in Germany, which was largely destroyed during the so-called Reichskristallnacht, or Night of the Broken Glass (9 November 1938) and since restored. A few days later, on September 9, to mark the Jewish New Year, the Charlottenburger Pestalozzistraße synagogue is also reopened. It is in this context that Heinz Galinski, president of Berlin's Jewish Community, expresses his regret that all efforts to find a successor for Rabbi Peter Levinson, who has returned to the United States, have failed so far due to the negative attitude of the Jewish world towards Jews in Germany. The Jewish community in Berlin, which numbered nearly 170,000 members before the outbreak of the Second World War, now, in 1953, stands at scarcely 7,000 faithful. To date, 7 of the 22 synagogues in Berlin that were either razed to the ground or, at the very least, severely damaged during the Night of the Broken Glass, have been rebuilt.

29 September 1953
Berlin mourns Ernst Reuter

He was Berlin's best ambassador, or at least the most loved, during the dark times that fell upon this city. During the blockade, with his famous beret and walking stick, he appealed to all the great political leaders in the free world to provide support and aid for Berlin. The mayor of Berlin, Ernst Reuter, has died from acute bronchitis at the age of 64 years in his apartment in Zehlendorfer Bülowstraße.

Riot police form a guard of honour flank Ernst Reuter's coffin at Schöneberg Town Hall.

The burial took place at the Zehlendorfer Waldfriedhof cemetery.

Thousands of Berliners mourned Reuter's death.

News of Reuter's untimely demise causes consternation and sadness amongst the Berlin population in both sides of the city. Spontaneously, many Berliners place candles in the windows of their homes, a gesture reminiscent of Reuter's own call for the people to light candles in remembrance of the prisoners of war who had still not returned home at Christmas 1952. On October 1, a funeral service takes place in the chamber of representatives, and the next day, hundreds of thousands of Berliners pass before Schöneberg Town Hall to pay their last respects to Berlin's most popular mayor. After the funeral rites, the coffin is carried by a ceremonial cortege through crowded streets – around one million Berliners turn out to say their last farewell to Reuter – to the Waldfriedhof Zehlendorf cemetery, where the burial takes place amongst family and friends (at a later ceremony, the name of one of the largest squares in Berlin, Charlottenburger Platz, known as Am Knie, is changed to Ernst-Reuter-Platz).

18 November 1953
Germany's best-known tabloid returns

For the first time since the end of the war, the newspaper BZ (*Berliner Zeitung*) is printed once more. Previously, the US High Commissioner, Ambassador James B. Conant, had made this possible by ordering the American commander-in-chief in Berlin, Thomas S. Timbermann, to grant the publishing company Ullstein a licence to produce an illustrated daily paper.
Berlin's political parties and newspaper publishers had expressed their opposition to this licence being granted to BZ. The fear was that a tabloid paper of this kind might exercise a negative influence over morale amongst Berlin's population as the city fights for freedom and independence.

The publisher Rudolf Ullstein and his nephew Karl (left) with a copy of the new BZ, dated 19.11.1953.

The front page of BZ. First edition since the end of the war, dated 18.11.1953.

Go West. Life on the "island"

17 September 1954
The Berlin Boulevard Berlin during
the Fourth International Film Festival

The three divas of European
cinema:

Gina Lollobrigida (right),
Sophia Loren (left) and, in
the middle, Yvonne de Carlo.

The most beautiful women in European cinema and some of the
most famous Hollywood stars bewitch the city. Festival fever
comes to Berlin, with countless filmstars suddenly within touching
distance. On the Kurfürstendamm, at the best restaurants and in
the renowned nightclubs, ordinary Berliners can, for once,
breathe in the aroma of beauty and originality, wealth and success. Crowds gather around the theatres where films are premiered. Amid these throngs, the stars they adore tread red
carpets on their way to take up their seats as their fans shout
out their admiration.

17 September 1954
The United States donates the most modern
library in Europe to Berlin

The United States spares no effort in helping West Berliners to
acquire a sense of democracy. The Amerika-Gedenkbibliothek opens
in Kreuzberger Blücherplatz. This American Memorial Library is big
enough to become Berlin's Central Library. It has been paid for by
donations from the American people, who have collected 5.4 mil-

lion marks to establish this great cultural facility in Berlin. No fewer than 110,000 volumes, worth 800,000 marks, are available for loan from this library, whilst music lovers will find a huge collection of records, sheet music and scores. Users can listen to discs in soundproofed booths. The magazine section stocks copies of more than 1,000 publications. The main storeroom, in the basement, is equipped with electrical goods lifts to carry books up and down, and holds up to 600,000 volumes. It is particularly stressed that, in making this gift, the North American people sought to commemorate what the people of Berlin had gone through and the courage they had shown during the blockade.

14 May 1955
GDR signs Warsaw Pact

On this day, presided over by the Soviet Union, eight East European states come together in Warsaw to form a military alliance. The Warsaw Pact is created as a counterweight to NATO, which is dominated by the United States.

12 July 1955
Berlin, the greenest and dampest city in Germany

This is a time when half Berlin takes to the road to enjoy the summer months. By train, by coach, on bicycles or noisy motorbikes and mopeds, Berliners move out to seek greener pastures and the waterside. And there are plenty of both, for there is no other city in all Germany with more green areas nor more rivers, canals and lakes. The beaches are packed, and the picnic areas are crowded, all tables occupied, with more and more chairs being added.

The American Memorial Library, or Amerika-Gedenkbibliothek (AGB): 70,000 books from the Berlin Dahlem Central Scientific Library are transferred to the new site in Blücherplat.

"Put on your swimsuit and get your little sister. We're going to the Wannsee right now ..."

Go West. Life on the "island"

The air in the city centre, which appears deserted on this Sunday morning, is still. The tarmac in the streets around Alexanderplatz is boiling. In Ku'damm, the waiters yawn before empty bars.

8 September 1955

The lost army

With joy and fear... In the arms of the father they believed dead: one of thousands released from Russian captivity long after the end of the war.

On this day, Federal Chancellor Konrad Adenauer inspects a company of honour during his visit to Moscow. He is received by Soviet president Nikolai Bulganin. In exchange for Adenauer's agreement to establish diplomatic relations, the Soviets free their remaining 9,226 prisoners. They have no further need for them.

Whist the Federal Republic prospers and begins to form a new army, despite opposition both within the country and abroad, thousands of soldiers from Hitler's army continue to vegetate in Soviet POW camps. For these last prisoners, the Second World War will not end until autumn 1955 when, ten years after German capitulation, they can return to a home they no longer recognise. Some 30% out of the 3.3 million German prisoners of war in the Soviet Union lose their lives there.

1 May 1956

Beer, cereals and sandwiches:
Berliners are what they eat

At the Hardtke restaurant, where the finest dishes in Berlin
are cooked and served, three customers discuss the food on
the menu. The French diner smiles. He considers it would be
going too far to call Berlin cuisine refined. But if only it were...
Berlin cuisine is not even original. It is just like the typical
Berliner: robust and reasonably generous. Pork hocks with
Sauerkraut, pickled cabbage and mashed peas and potatoes,
Kassler pork loin with cabbage and mashed peas or carob
soup... sweet and sour kidneys, with mashed potatoes, of
course.
In Aschinger am Zoo, there is plenty of pea soup with bread. All
for 50 Pfennigs. It has been this way for nearly 30 years now:
Berliners can never get enough. But what is most fashionable in
Berlin is snack culture.
Today, the four most glorious snacks – meatballs, *bockwurst*,
pickled gherkins and pickled eggs – have an outsider to contend
with: the *currywurst* sausage. This new snack has been all the
rage amongst Berliners since exactly 4 September 1949, when
Herta Heuwer, owner of a hotdog stand in Stuttgarter Platz, got
bored because she had very few customers that day. So she
decided to experiment a little, and the result is a sausage cut
into slices, covered in ketchup, Worcester sauce, curry powder
and paprika. This concoction is soon found all over the city, but
generally in the form of poor imitations, as Frau Heuwer has kept
the secret of her sauce to herself.

For my French friend, a
Bouillon á la Erbse...

At Maitre Aschangier, more
simply known as Aschinger,
Berlin's most popular fast
food restaurant.

Go West. Life on the "island"

19 September 1956
Queues at emergency camps

One of the thousands of refugees from the Soviet-controlled zone at the Berlin-Marienfelde transit camp.

These are days when thousands of people often wait outside the Marienfelde and Lankwitz camps in West Berlin to register as refugees from the GDR and apply for political asylum. The president, Willy Brandt, addresses Berlin's house of representatives to remind members about the national tragedy that is reflected in the numbers of those leaving the GDR (the next day, September 20, sees the arrival of the one millionth refugee).

The Senate report "Germans take refuge amongst Germans" notes that 6,785 homes had been built for refugees by the end of 1953, and that a further 575 have been completed to date, in 1956. This means that Berlin can provide homes for around 32,000 refugees, most of whom have been granted asylum by the Federal Republic.

1957
Willy Brandt elected mayor

Berlin's chamber of representatives elects the president of the parliament, 43-year-old Willy Brandt, as the city's new mayor. He succeeds Otto Suhr, who died on August 30 at the age of 63. Willy Brandt was born in Lübeck on 18 December 1913 under the name of Herbert Frahm. An active member of the SPD, he was forced to flee to Scandinavia when the Nazis came to power (Ernst Reuter, very much a model, fled from the Nazis to Turkey), Frahm changed his name to Willy Brandt. In 1936, Brandt spent a few months in Berlin, where he ran an underground resistance movement (for which reason, after the war, former Nazis reviled him as a traitor). In 1938, having gone into exile, he obtained Norwegian nationality. A journalist by profession, Brandt continued his work of combating the Nazis, firstly in Norway and later in Sweden, right up to the end of the war.

Brandt returned to his native Germany in 1945. After working as a correspondent for several Scandinavian newspapers and for the Norwegian military mission to West Berlin, he once more adopted German nationality. Joining the SPD, he sat as a member of parliament for Berlin since he was first elected in 1949. One of Ernst Reuter's closest collaborators, he became the leader of the Berlin SPD on the mayor's death. Willy Brandt became known for his position in the party as one of those most committed to forging closer ties with the western alliance and the Allied Powers.

After the great Ernst Reuter, Willy Brandt was to become Berlin's most popular mayor-president.

The president of Berlin's house of representatives is elected mayor.

26 October 1958

Rock around the clock

What a picture: pomaded quiff, long hair combed back to create the famous pompadour look. Legs clad in American blue denim jeans, torso bedecked with black leather bomber jacket.

Rock'n'roll as a way of life, 24 hours a day.

The demolished sports palace.

The shirt studiously unbuttoned. A chain hangs from the chest... what is this leaning over the silver jukebox? A hooligan! One of the thousands that today smashed up their chairs at the sports palace during a concert by North American rock'n'roll singer Bill Haley.

Hundreds of young people storm the stage, followed by the police. A real battle breaks out in the hall. The rebellious crowd attack the forces of order with chair legs. A total of 17 people are seriously injured, another hundred or so suffer bumps and bruises.

In the future, there will be no more rock'n'roll events at this venue. Similar disturbances had already occurred at the concert given here by the popular American singer Johnny Ray on March 29.

6 July 1959
George Grosz dies

The Berlin-born painter George Grosz.

This Berlin painter was considered a star amongst artists. After the First World War, few painters have expressed their critical vision of society with such conviction. George Grosz dedicated his entire work to the great city of Moloch, to the war wounded returning from the front, to the bankers who had stayed at home, to judges and attorneys, to the legions of nameless servants and working-class people. As a member of the November Group, founded in Berlin in 1918, Grosz was a key figure in the new naturalism that was just beginning to emerge.

What really happened on 13 August 1961?

13 August 1961
Berlin is divided into two

It is just after midnight. In the dark, strange movements are seen along the rows of houses that line the streets in the eastern part of the city closest to the border with the Soviet-occupied sector. These, the latest to return from captivity witness strange goings-on. At 1.11 in the morning, the GDR news agency, ADN, sends out an announcement from the Warsaw Pact governments recommending "close surveillance and effective control" of the frontier with West Berlin. Shortly after 2 am, the first barbed-wire fences are erected near Potsdamer Platz. By around 3.30 am, barriers have been placed along the entire border between the two sectors. Streets are dug up and closed off by concrete posts or road blocks. A growing number of People's Army armoured car columns head for the border.
The first news of these road blocks reaches West Berlin at around 2 am. The police are placed on alert.

Construction of the Berlin Wall in November 1961: military and construction vehicles around the section at the Brandenburg Gate.

What really happened on 13 August 1961?

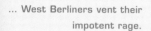

... West Berliners vent their impotent rage.

Demonstration against the construction of the Wall. Banner-wielding young people protest at the Brandenburg Gate.

Meanwhile, West Germany has other concerns: the electoral campaign has got under way. Willy Brandt, mayor of West Berlin and leader of the SPD Social Democratic Party is not in the city. At this moment, he is travelling in a special carriage that his party has had attached to the regular Nuremberg-Kiel express. However, he is wakened just an hour after the first signs of unusual movement by the Berlin police are noted. Brandt continues to Hanover, where he takes the first flight back to Berlin, reaching Tempelhof Airport at 8.55 am. Without pause, he then makes his way as quickly as possible to the Brandenburg Gate.

(Much later, those with the mayor of Berlin that day still remember the shock that fell over everyone present; stunned, Brandt viewed a scene he does not want to believe, but which is the pure truth). Brandt quickly returns and immediately calls for a special session of the senate, which begins minutes later, at 9.30 am. Konrad Adenauer, who had also been awoken during the night, carries on sleeping until morning, as those in his circle later recall. It would appear that he does not consider it necessary to interrupt his electoral campaign that Sunday, August 13 to make for Berlin with all haste. But for Willy Brandt, who looks all around to find friends of Berlin prepared to back him up all the way, this is just the first of the many disappointments that await him. At around 12.40, angry Berliners begin to pull down the barbed-wire fences around the Tiergarten Park. The People's Police send guards, their bayonets at the ready. At 1.55 pm, a man trying to escape from East Berlin is arrested by three police officers. He somehow manages to grab one policeman's weapon and continue to flee, but the *Vopos* stop him and pin him to the ground inside West Berlin territory. At almost the same time, another four men and three women escape along the Teltow Canal.

What really happened on 13 August 1961?

The people of West Berlin threaten to attack the People's Police from various points. Stories about attempts to escape, some successful and others foiled, arrived from all along the border between the two sectors. At 4.01 pm, West Berliners try to remove the barbed-wire blockade in Swinemünder Straße. The *Vopos* are vociferously booed when they mount machine gun posts in the street. At 8 pm, some East German Border Guards start to use tear gas and smoke bombs. West Berliners respond by throwing stones. Soon after this, the *Vopos* let five East Berliners climb onto the barbed-wire fences in Alte Jakobstraße and then look the other way when they pass into the West through the gap they have made. At 9 pm, West Berlin police spring into action for the first time, breaking up a demonstration against the GDR regime that has assembled in Straße des 17 Juni. The last newsflash of the day goes out at 0.10 am: West Berlin police authorities report large-scale vehicle movements around the Brandenburg Gate. Russian security forces have been reinforced around the monument in honour of the Soviets. Fear begins to spread all over the city.

This August 13, Willy Brandt's struggle is in vain

Whilst many East Berliners try to escape to the West, and West Berliners attempt to control their rage against the border guards, the members of the People's Army and the *Vopos*, in the political field Willy Brandt is confronted by fresh disappointment.

The inhabitants of Bernauer Straße, in the Wedding district, flee their homes with the little they can carry, to get to West Berlin, which begins on the pavement opposite their homes.

What really happened on 13 August 1961?

Forced evacuation of houses in Harzer Straße. Watched by People's Police officers, furniture is loaded onto removals lorries.

Approaching the Allied commanders of West Berlin as the city's mayor-president, Brandt is given an ice-cold reception. Nonetheless, he shows great self-control.

"What happened last night is a violation of the treaty signed by the four powers for free movement throughout Berlin", he begins, "The Soviet Union has divided Berlin by an administrative measure. The Warsaw Pact nations have declared their solidarity with the USSR. For this reason, the West must lodge a complaint, not only with Moscow, but before all the Warsaw Pact capitals." The Allied commanders of West Berlin have nothing to say. As will become clear, they are not even convinced that the entire population of Berlin shares Brandt's concern. They are not at all keen to alarm their governing bodies in Paris, London and Washington. This much, at least, is clear. And, moreover, it is Sunday, and it is still night-time in Washington. Willy Brandt annoys them with his "lack of respect." He is so impolite, so upset, he can hardly contain himself... everything that a politician should not be or do.

He even shouts at them in English, the language they speak. They explain to him that they cannot do anything, because they have received no orders, neither from Washington nor from London or Paris (how could they receive orders, if the West has yet to be informed about the catastrophe that has taken place?).

Brandt is deeply upset (though he does not know at the time that the Western Powers are powerless to do anything immediately. He does not know that the Soviets will seal the division of the city at lightning speed, whilst the Western Powers continue, basically, to do nothing). At first, the mayor of Berlin is the only person in a position of authority to react as everyone should have reacted. More than 2,300,000 people gather before his government office, Schöneberg City Hall, to find out what is going on and what is to become of their city.

16 August 1961
Willy Brandt's vain appeal

Brandt needs to give heart to the people. But how? What should he, what could he, promise them (later on, his intimates will recall that he was angry, desperate, it was plain to all, and with good reason). He could not even deny stories that had appeared in the newspapers that, quite correctly as it was to turn out, voice the suspicion that the Americans would finally accept this obvious injustice. The mayor needs to encourage the population, yet neither should he inflame their feelings too much. He cannot urge them to revolt, as in that case they will attack the border posts, and the Soviets will send tanks into action. Then all will really be lost. The speech he finally gives to the crowd is perhaps the most difficult one he has delivered to date or ever will. It is also his most desperate, at least that is what he feels when he ends. Later on, his staff will recall that he was completely drenched in sweat and that his hands and knees were shaking.

But, even more than West Berliners, it was East Berliners who feel betrayed, sold out. But both have been caught in a trap, the same trap, though each on different sides.

"How can we console ...?" Willy Brandt's speech outside Schöneberg City Hall.

What really happened on 13 August 1961?

19 August 1961
People throw themselves from windows

Bernauer Straße: East Berliner Frieda Schultze (Granny Schultze), 77, flees to the West through her window. West Berlin firemen wait below to break her fall in a rescue blanket.

But not everyone jumps successfully. On August 22, a 58-year-old woman falls to her death.

On this day, People's Police officers and members of the SED combat groups erect barricades outside doors and windows on ground-floor houses along Schwedter and Brunnenstraße streets. Here, the rows of houses form the border with West Berlin's Wedding district. Two days later, the inhabitants are forced to leave their homes hurriedly. Next, the windows are bricked up. The inhabitants of 7, Bernauer Straße jump to safety from a fourth floor into the rescue blanket held by West Berlin firemen.

It is September 24 and Frieda Schultze, 77 years of age, has decided to jump to the West. People's Police have stormed her house to try to stop her. She is hanging from the wall of her house and no one on the West Berlin pavement can help her.

22 October 1961

Third world war threatens to break out at Checkpoint Charlie

Nightfall marks the start of a four-day period that will be tense in the extreme. Berlin is like an enormous powder keg rolling faster and faster, whilst its fuse comes closer and closer to being lit.

Since August 13, Berlin has been shaken by bad news every day. One crisis occurs and disappears again, almost without trace, whilst the next one, even more laden with doom, begins to raise its head. Over the course of these hours, days, weeks, many compare the city with an avalanche of ever-larger problems that will finally come crashing down at the foot of a mountain built from hope and rational thought, radically changing the current political and social panorama.

Like the two world wars and many other dramatic moments in history, the crisis that occurs on this night of October 22 begins as the result of a banal, everyday event: the American ambassador, Allan Lightner, wants to cross the border at Checkpoint Charlie with his wife to go to the opera in the Eastern section.

Checkpoint Charlie is the only point at which the Allies can cross over.

Contravening the rules agreed with the Allies, a border guard asks Lightner for his identity papers. This enrages the ambassador, for uniformed Allied personnel from the four powers can travel between all sectors in the city freely and without being challenged.

The allied border post at Checkpoint Charlie.

What really happened on 13 August 1961?

The American ambassador's refusal to show his documentation to the GDR border guard is totally justified. Believing that the sentry is merely ignorant of Allied regulations, Lightner demands to speak with a Soviet officer, but the guard refuses to inform his superior. And the US Secretary for Foreign Affairs, alarmed, comes close to accepting this new rule, inspired by Soviet desperation. That is what would have happened if, in 1948, General Clay, responding to the Soviet blockade with the Air Lift, had not immediately informed President Kennedy. If the United States gave in, the Soviets would soon take control over the roads, too, reasoned Clay, who defended his standpoint with such conviction that Kennedy stood by his general.

25 October 1961
The world powers prepare for war

At 8.30 am, US jeeps and tanks are deployed at Checkpoint Charlie, which is now manned by elite soldiers dress in combat uniform. A high-ranking American officer walks to the demarcation line and negotiates with the similarly high ranking officer who comes up to him. Failing to reach an agreement, the two men separate once more.

American tanks, as seen by the Soviets, at Checkpoint Charlie.

What really happened on 13 August 1961?

Soviet tanks, from the US viewpoint.

Soviet tanks stand on one side of Checkpoint Charlie, faced by US Army tanks on the other side.

At 10.45, two US officers, accompanied by twelve soldiers carrying guns, bayonets at the ready, drive up to the barrier. The convoy is allowed to enter the Soviet sector without resistance. After a brief incursion a few metres into enemy territory, the vehicle stops, turns and returns to West Berlin. However, at 2.15 pm, an American bus carrying military and civil personnel is turned back from the border post. Once more, the order is given to show their identification, and once more, this demand is refused. Meanwhile, the Americans have positioned several tanks along the Friedrichstraße.

The Soviets react to this deployment by placing another 30 tanks of their own opposite the US tanks. Tension is increasing. For the first time, 16 years after the capitulation of the German empire, the two great world powers, allies in the Second World War, confront each other as enemies at Checkpoint Charlie on Berlin's Friedrichstraße. The "sovereignty" that the Soviets and the GDR authorities have been at such pains to stress now bursts like a soap bubble. The world, which had been holding its breath, understands that the "workers' and farmers' state" is a puppet dancing to the tune the Soviets play.

More and more people, in Germany and all over the world, are expressing their fear that the third world war may eventually break out here. And indeed, it is a close thing. People flock from all over the western districts, full of fear, terror, anger and resentment. They want to see the unbelievable with their own eyes in order to attempt to understand it.

And they shout encouragement at their protectors, though they are the ones most in need of encouragement. They share the little they have, even the little hope that remains to them...

To the surprise of all observers, the tense situation de-escalates. Khrushchev withdraws the Soviet tanks without comment. What has made the Russian leader take this unexpected decision? What has happened in the wings? Have the Western Powers successfully blackmailed the Soviets?
Khrushchev had kept himself fully informed about the situation at Checkpoint Charlie.
(Later on, Khrushchev will give an explanation to his closest circles. His reasoning, entirely logical, is as follows: "Everybody knows that tanks go backwards and forwards. If they had gone forward, it would have meant war... But West Berlin is not important to us, so I ordered our tanks to withdraw").

Over the eight weeks leading up to the construction of the Wall, Khrushchev had been playing poker and he had dealt himself a winning hand. His judgement had been proved correct on all counts, even most recently, when he wagered that the Western Powers would finally accept the construction of the Wall, despite their vociferous protests. At least, as long as their right to move freely around the city, without control, was not restricted.
As regards the rules for Checkpoint Charlie, the four victorious powers soon reached an agreement to the effect that, in future, Allied personnel in civilian dress need only show their identification papers from their vehicle window. Other types of control would not be imposed.

What really happened on 13 August 1961?

The origins behind the construction of the Wall

Above all, the construction of the Wall brought the series of crises that had followed the blockade to an end. The origins of its construction, according to most researchers into the subject, do not lie in any desire to "guarantee peace", but in the GDR's knee-jerk reaction to the urgent need to stem the constant flow of de refugees fleeing from East Germany. The construction of the Wall is the GDR's confession that, after 40 years of continuous experimentation, the regime had failed both socially and economically.

When the frontier between the German Democratic Republic and the Federal Republic of Germany was closed in 1952, Berlin was the only place to which East Germans could any longer escape. The status of the four occupying powers guaranteed freedom of residence within the city limits. In the eyes of the Soviet Union government, this was a serious hindrance to the USSR's attempts to consolidate its power within its sphere of influence. The massive numbers of citizens fleeing the country made the GDR regime fear for its very existence. After the Soviet ultimatum in 1958 calling on the Western Powers to leave Berlin had expired without persuading the Allies to leave the city, and in view of the fact that the GDR's situation showed little sign of improving, Walter Ulbricht, first secretary of state on the SED Central Committee, insisted on a violent solution: Berlin should be taken by military means. However, Nikita Khrushchev, the Soviet president, rejected this proposal. Due to the dangerous tension between the Soviet Union and China, the Communist Bloc needed at all costs to avoid direct confrontation with the USA.

The GDR was clearly threatened with economic and social disintegration. The secretaries general of the Warsaw Pact states communist parties decided to negotiate. They chose the safest option: to build the Wall. Unlike Berlin's mayor, Willy Brandt, they already knew that the Western Powers had decided to accept this measure without protest.

Wave of GDR refugees: 1949-1962

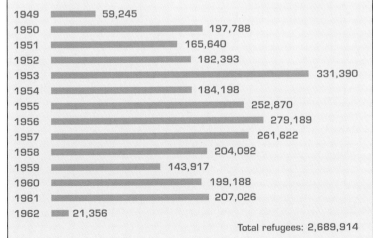

Year	Refugees
1949	59,245
1950	197,788
1951	165,640
1952	182,393
1953	331,390
1954	184,198
1955	252,870
1956	279,189
1957	261,622
1958	204,092
1959	143,917
1960	199,188
1961	207,026
1962	21,356

Total refugees: 2,689,914

Total population: 17.2 million (1960). Source: Federal Statistics Service

Walled in

Hope under the hammer, the compass and the laurel wreath

17 August 1962

Peter Fechter shot dead

East Berlin border guards shoot 18-year-old Peter Fechter as he tries to escape to the West. Dying from his wounds, the young man is left lying behind the wall in East Berlin territory. West Berlin police look on impotently as the boy slowly bleeds to death.

The tragic event occurs at around 2 pm. Fechter, a building worker in Unter den Linden, had tried to get over the Wall from Zimmerstraße, near Checkpoint Charlie, along with a workmate. Though his companion had managed to successfully jump to the West, Fechter was hit by shots fired by GDR border guards. He fell back into East Berlin with one bullet in his stomach and another in his lungs.

The emblem of the German Democratic Republic (GDR).

The architecture of the murderous, crazy desire for dominance: the Berlin Wall in Bernauer Straße.

Walled in

Peter Fechter

He slowly bled to death from bullet wounds in his stomach and lungs.

It was 50 minutes after he was shot that the fatally wounded young man was finally removed by GDR border guards.

West Berlin police arrive, climbing up onto the wall. They throw bandages to the seriously wounded young man, but dare not cross over to the other side. On the East Berlin side, no one offers help. Peter Fechter lies just behind the wall amongst the barbed wire and other barricades.

People gather on both sides of the wall, hearing the youth's cries for help. In West Berlin, the police contain the furious crowd only with difficulty.

West Berliners shout insults and threats at the GDR border guards: "murderers, criminals!" They respond by firing tear gas. The West Berlin police respond in kind, also firing tear gas, and an obscene duel breaks out as Fechter bleeds to death.

The incident causes a wave of indignation in West Berlin. Throughout the night and over the following days, demonstrations take place, accompanied by violent rioting.

26 June 1963

East Berliners cheer Kennedy visit

On his visit to Germany, US President John F. Kennedy stops off for eight hours in Berlin. In East Berlin, countless people sit behind firmly closed windows and doors in front of their radios, the volume turned down low. Most listen with all ears to the report broadcast by the RiaS, banned in the East. At about 9.40 am, the president's airplane touches down at Tegel Airport, where John F. Kennedy is welcomed by the Federal Chancellor,

Konrad Adenauer, and the mayor of the city, Willy Brandt, as well as the three Allied commanders in West Berlin. The President's retinue includes the US Secretary of State, Dean Rusk, and the former military governor of Germany – a hero to all Berliners – General Lucius D. Clay. In his open car, Kennedy begins a 52-kilometre tour of West Berlin, welcomed by a crowd of 1,400,000 cheering people.

John F. Kennedy visits Checkpoint Charlie.

"Ich bin ein Berliner!" ("I am a Berliner!").

Kennedy's famous words, which also encouraged East Berliners, were dictated by a German journalist and written phonetically on a note passed to the president (as was later revealed).

Kennedy's visit culminates in his speech before 400,000 Berliners outside Schöneberg City Hall. The president ends with a short phrase in German (which he reads from a note handed to him): "Ich bin ein Berliner!" ("I am a Berliner!").
At a reception that evening, the Free University confers the distinction of favourite son on Kennedy. Once more, he takes this opportunity not only to support the people of Berlin's desire for freedom, but also to promote understanding with the East.

18 December 1963
Safe conducts for West Berlin

All Berliners are pleased. An agreement has been signed for a "small" regulation governing safe conducts. For the first time since the building of the Wall, West Berliners can enter the other part of the city. From December 18 to January 4, it is possible to request a pass a schools in the twelve western districts to be handed to post office officials in East Berlin. Once applications have been processed by East Berlin, West Berliners

Walled in

57 people make a mass escape from Bernauer Straße:

Two children outside the house, now cordoned off, where the tunnel entrance was found.

A woman is pulled along by cables through the tunnel from 97, Bernauer Straße 97 (West Berlin) to Strelitzer Straße (East Berlin).

will receive one-day passes, as long as officials in the East have no objection.

When at 1 pm today, December 18, the safe conduct offices open, thousands of applications are received (over the Christmas period alone, some 150,000 West Berliners take the chance to visit relatives in the East).

5 October 1964

Spectacular tunnel escape

In what is the biggest tunnel break-out since the Wall was built, 57 East Berliners manage to escape to the West. When soldiers patrolling the frontier between the two sectors of the city turn their attention on those helping them to get away, shooting begins and a GDR border guard is killed.

Those who escape unhurt are 25 men and 31 women, along with three children aged from three to seven years. They had dragged themselves along the tunnel in various groups on the evening of October 3. The tunnel, 150 metres long, later blocked off, runs from 97, Bernauer Straße, in Wedding district, to a lean-to in Strelitzer Straße, in East Berlin.

The underground escape route was dug by a dozen students who had already fled to West Berlin, and who started the work in April. Up to 11 metres deep, the tunnel is between 50 and 80 centimetres in diameter.

At around 12.30 am on October 5, just before the great escape was due to end, three GDR soldiers see four people, armed with pistols, helping the last fugitives to flee along the hidden tunnel.

Shooting breaks out, and GDR frontier guard Egon Schultz is killed by a shot from his own comrades.

Whilst the GDR authorities speak of "deliberate murder", official reports in West Berlin describe the incident as the result of legitimate self-defence.

5 May 1971
Walter Ulbricht resigns

Power changes hands:

Walter Ulbricht (left) with Erich Honecker (right).

Walter Ulbricht resigns as general secretary of the SED Central Committee, handing the post on to Erich Honecker, a member of the SED politburo since 1956 and at the time the Central Committee member responsible for security.

According to the official account, Ulbricht resigns as party leader due to reasons of age, though he will continue in the post as president of the State Council and, therefore, nominal GDR head of state. The apprentice cabinet maker is replaced by the roofer's apprentice. Ulbricht joined the German Communist Party (KPD) in 1919 and was elected to parliament in 1928. In 1933, he left Germany, living for a time in France before settling in the Soviet Union. He became leader of the SED in 1946, organising the party under the Soviet model. In 1950, he was appointed General Secretary of the SED (becoming First Secretary in 1953) and in 1960 he rose to the position of president of the GDR State Council.

Walled in

17 August 1972
The young rebel in niches

Art as a weapon against the lethargy that reigns in the number one "Cinderella state": disaffected draughtsmen, artists and painters. Crazy hairdressers and out-of-control photographers with models completely off their heads. Their motto: *Go West*. But the goal of these "disaffected" young people is driven by the desire to imitate behaviour in Western late capitalist society, something frowned on by most of the population still; rather, it is the idea of freedom that spurs them on. However, the party demands more than robot obedience: it also wants to govern what people think.

28 March 1973
The SED Entertainment Committee seeks to put young people back on the "right track"

The SED sets up the Entertainment Committee in order to bring the music industry into line. Already, in 1965, Walter Ulbricht, president of the GDR State Council, had criticised the beat music that was popular in the West, seeing in these new rhythms an "attempt by western imperialist agents to lead the GDR to arm itself for a noise war." As far as possible, the SED prohibited all Western influences, whether musical, fashion or youth culture. But not even when allowed to wear local made bomber jackets and imitation jeans would young people do as the FDJ wished. Again and again, young people caused scandals, again and again they were disciplined or punished for their ideas, which were reflected in their very look.

Undesirable "Birds of Paradise".

14 March 1984

The "border of death" is perfected for
the coming decades

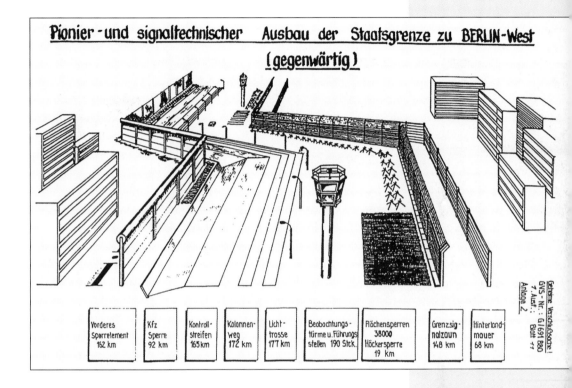

Pionier-und signaltechnischer Ausbau der Staatsgrenze zu BERLIN-West (gegenwärtig)

| Vorderes Sperrelement 162 km | Kfz Sperre 92 km | Kontroll- streifen 165 km | Kolonnen- weg 172 km | Licht- trasse 177 km | Beobachtungs- türme u. Führungs- stellen 190 Stck. | Flächensperren 38000 Höckersperre 19 km | Grenzsig- nalzaun 148 km | Hinterland- mauer 68 km |

Geheime Verschlußsache!
GVS - Nr.: G 1691 880
7. Ausf.:
Blatt 11
Anlage 2

The GDR regime organises for decades to come. Between the
Brandenburg Gate and Potsdam Square, GDR border guards
continue to modernise their systems along the frontier, building a
second wall which runs parallel to the divide through the city centre. On 16 August 1961, work begins to replace the barbed-wire
fencing with a wall as the border with West Berlin becomes more
and more impregnable.
By the 1970s, the 165.7-kilometre border with West Berlin is
defended by a complex system of walls, tracks and anti-vehicle
blocks.

Berlin Wall System and
Signage on the Border with
West Berlin

• Main concrete wall: 162 km
• Anti-vehicle ditches: 92 km
• Patrol tracks: 165 km
• Vehicle patrol track: 172 km
• Illuminated control areas:
  177 km
• Watch towers and command
  posts: 190
• Barrier blocks: 38,000
• Anti-tank barriers: 19 km
• Border signal fence: 148 km
• Inner wall: 68 km

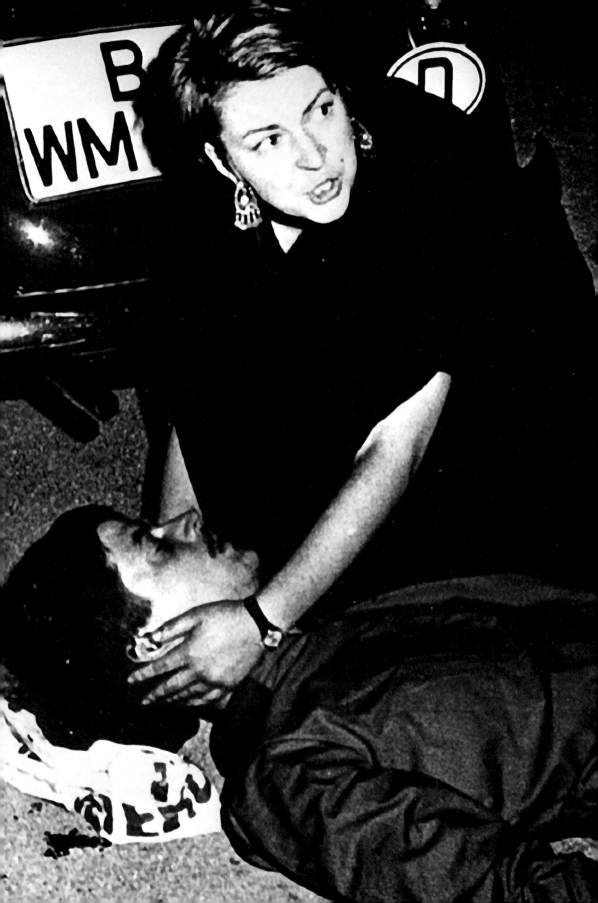

On the "island"

Generally speaking, the elders feel most satisfied with themselves. As has occurred all over West Germany, in West Berlin too people have got down to work in an orderly fashion to produce the economic miracle. Savings accounts, cars, holidays in Italy, nice houses with indoor palm trees, hi-fi equipment, built-in cookers... At last they can afford things again.

Life on the "island" that is West Berlin would be truly a model of good order were it not for the enormous disorder that reigns amongst young people who, rather than getting on with their studying, prefer to try to put the world to rights: daydreamers who shout "Yanks Out of Vietnam" in the streets, whilst at home they enrage their parents with cheeky questions about what they did when Hitler was in power.

The anger of sons and the scorn of daughters towards their "elders and betters" exploded suddenly... or did it? Perhaps this sudden noisy outbreak by the young is nothing more than a logical reaction to the long silence of their parents.

June 1961
Film festival's first scandal a great popular hit

The film festival this year shows up the generation of Germans who "escaped with their lives once more" for the puritans they are by featuring the American actress Jane Mansfield, whose screen presence can clearly only be gauged using a tape measure.

At last, instead of explosive and incendiary bombs, Berlin shakes to the impact caused by a posse of sex bombs led by Jane Mansfield.

The festival director, Alfred Bauer, angrily complains that: "Shameless display of the North American actress Jane Mansfield's physical charms is considered inappropriate and wrong..." Berlin, a den of inequity? However that may be, festival fans are delighted.

1 October 1961
Nazi criminals freed

Having served their 20-year sentences, with remission, Albert Speer, the Third Reich Arms Minister, and Baldur von Schirach, former Nazi Youth leader, are freed from the Allied prison for war prisoners in Spandau, Berlin.

Albert Speer, former Third Reich Minister for Arms and War Production, after release from prison, meets the press at the Hotel Gerhus in Berlin-Grunewald.

20 February 1963
At the theatre, a play accuses the Church

The Freie Volksbühne, near Kurfürstendamm, premieres Rolf Hochhuth's play *The Deputy*. Erwin Piscator directs this provocative drama in which Hochhuth makes the Pope, leader of the Catholic Church, partly responsible for the Nazi extermination of the Jews. By exploring a subject so controversial and explosive that no one had dared bring it up before, Piscator deliberately awakens memories of the theatrical scandals that affected many careers in the 1920s. The problems begin with work preparing the production of this play, as yet unpublished and subtitled *A Christian Tragedy*, as a provisional legal ban has been placed on its performance, with all the financial risks this entails.

Rolf Hochhuth's play The Deputy is premiered at the Freie Volksbühne in Berlin.

Günter Tabor, who plays Riccardo, with Erhard Stettner as "the old man" and Richard Häussler as "Doctor Sacha Berger".

Preparations for the first night are accompanied by the publication of short extracts and passages from the thick, 200-page bundle of documents which Hochhuth has assembled to defend the historical bases for his play. The Catholic Church wastes no time in responding. *Petrusblatt*, official publication of the Berlin bishopric, furiously enters the debate. Five days before the play is due to open, Berlin's Catholic Committee sends out documentary material to all theatre critics in the city, as well as to the television, radio and press, containing allegations against which Hochhuth is forced to defend his play. Police protection is brought in, and spectators are requested not to express opinions of any kind before the play ends. There is silence throughout the performance, but once the curtain comes down the Berlin audience cheers and applauds the work loudly for several minutes.

20 May 1963
Berlin's lucky nighthawks

A Munich journalist is asked by his paper to file a report on the myth of Berlin's nightlife. The people of Munich will be amazed. The West Berlin that Bavarians usually either laugh at or feel sorry for, and which is only remembered for its inhabitants' traditional fame of having the gift of the gab, now boasts around 4,000 eateries. From the bar on the corner to the refined club with a sign saying "Right of Admission Reserved" on the door. Young people can choose from a limitless *menu* of night-time entertainment. The attractions include a host of deafening clubs and discotheques, many of them frequented by tourists known here as *Wessis*,

Cheznous bar and cabaret,
in Marburger Straße.
(Night-time view of the
exterior).

The British actor Peter
Ustinov (left) with friend,
talking on the phone at the
Resi dance hall.

because they soon give themselves away as "village oafs" with their comic dance styles. They might be from another planet as far as sophisticated Berlin tastes are concerned.

Berlin's first large discotheque, with its own live DJ, is the Big Apple in Bundesallee, which opens in 1962. A basement full of smoke and loud beat music haunted by the fashionable and writhing to the latest dance moves. Trendies also meet at the Riverboot, in Hohenzollerndamm. The austere stairs leading up to this great office block gives no clue to what goes on under its roof. Here there is a constant coming and going along the corridors of the vast halls where beat groups from London and Liverpool play. In between are silent oases where couples kiss under shady lights to the sound of catchy dance tunes.

Night time Casanovas, less attractive in the light of day, look forward to exciting evenings at the Resi de Hasenheide, a vast club, a veritable palace where orchestras and big bands perform. Here, 250 table telephones are ready to launch the attack. Water shows, using truly spectacular lighting effects, project different types of waterfalls onto the stage, consuming 8,000 litres of water per minute, whilst 6.5 kilometres of electrical cable provide 350,000 Watts of lighting, with nothing to envy of Las Vegas. The drag queen show at Cheznous is considered of the best in Europe, but there are drag queen shows all over Berlin, at parties everywhere, both in the rear buildings of the petit bourgeoisie and in the Dahlemer villas belonging to the rich. Berlin was always rather more Babylonian than Schwabing's bohemia could even dream of.

But Berlin is a favourite destination even for homosexuals rather less camp. The district around Nollendorfplatz is a world in itself. The first "clubs for men" opened around here in the time of

Emperor Wilhelm. At KC – the men's club with the strictest controls on admissions anywhere in Germany, and where the doorman would inspect all prospective clients carefully through the spyhole in the locked entrance door before deciding whether or not to open up – the demanding customer will find film and theatre actors, designers and male models, luxury callboys and beautiful strangers drawn here only by curiosity.

Drinks are served at the busy bar run by Jean Claude, the adopted son of the dancer Josephine Baker. At Le Punsch, everything is even more intimate and gay. This is Berlin's must original and unusual gay club, where women are allowed in, as long as they look interesting enough and their "references" are equally positive. Time and again, men feel as if they have suddenly woken up in the middle of a Carnival ball, saved from their permanent nightmare of bourgeois desolation. Until outside, at the door, at the summer dawn and for no apparent reason, once more a dozen shimmering transvestites and drag queens start hitting each other with their handbags, their wigs shaking and getting entangled with their earrings, shouting and screaming so much that the police turn up with various vehicles to take them all away, along with the customers they have ejected from Punsch, in Gothaer Straße, the return to "normal" life, though first each and every one of them must first allow themselves to be fingerprinted.

(The discriminatory "Article 175" on homosexuality will not be repealed until 1974, after the student riots. Until then, the Berlin police will raid their clubs and carry out random searches of "suspects").

Always lovely (and) decadent.

Berlin night-club: a group of transvestites varnishing their nails.

14 June 1963

A museum abhorred by the GDR opens at Checkpoint Charlie

Rainer Hildebrandt, imprisoned by the Nazis in 1944 for fighting with the resistance, freed at the end of the war to face an even more terrible and uncertain fate and since then a fighter against the GDR dictatorship with its systematic abuses of justice, today opens the Berlin Wall Museum, his own idea and initiative. It is said that many escape plans were hatched in the building that now houses the museum, and which stands right on the border, the infamous Checkpoint Charlie in Friedrichstraße, and that the disinterested people who help East Berliners to escape receive here the logistic support and even economic aid that they need.

Escape car with bullet holes.

Dr. Rainer Hildebrandt (second on the right) at a press conference with refugees from the GDR.

(For many people, the Wall Museum, threatened for years by GDR secret service agents, has become an island of hope amid a sea of desperation. Here, victims and saviours can meet; here, public talks and other events take place; here, guests of honour from all over the world are welcomed, and each guest of the city here learns about the unimaginable needs of the "walled in" ("Eingemauerten") and the persecuted with their escape attempts both successful and unsuccessful. What we can neither see nor touch, but which we can very much feel, is the desperation, the cold sweat and tears of the people whose struggles are immortalised here.

Apart from viewing documents, photographs and recordings that can only be seen in the museum, visitors will also be amazed by the exhibits featuring original equipment used to escape. Here, too, is the famous cable car, the hot-air balloon, the precariously-built light aircraft and the tiny converted car with its sophisticated hiding-place).

22 May 1965

The economic miracle in West Berlin

Businesses belonging neither to the hotel trade nor its suppliers are complaining once more. Whilst in West Germany generally, industry, the service sector and wholesale trade are booming, a shadow continues to hang over West Berlin, and the city's economy has to be artificially kick started by federal aid and tax breaks.

Half the blockaded city can hardly compete due to the employment situation, to the high cost of air transport and the difficulties surrounding other access routes. Very few West German companies open branches here. Growing industries, such as advertising agencies, cannot ask their demanding clientele to make the journey to Berlin, and therefore become concentrated in Düsseldorf, Hamburg and Frankfurt. The employment market in Berlin is "antiquated", and for this reason more and more young people are leaving the city. Berlin is in danger of becoming an old folk's home. The only sector flourishing is the tourist trade, with all that entails.

When one of Berlin's great street parties (which will later become known as the Love Parade, the Carnival of the Cultures and Christopher Street Day) is organised, hundreds of thousands of curious spectators and "insiders" flock to the city. And people still enjoy strolling along Ku'damm, 3,500 metres long and 53 metres wide. It takes at least two hours to walk along both sides of this great avenue, even a whole day. It depends on how much time and freedom the visitor has to look, wonder, browse, try, taste and purchase. The 200 or so buildings that line the avenue contain seven theatres and a score of restaurants, bars and cafés. And at least double that number of fashion boutiques, jewellers and other luxury goods establishments. Hotels, restaurants, discotheques, nightclubs brothels and the souvenir trade are all doing healthy business. Moreover, Berlin is the venue of many great events, congresses and international trade fairs. Finally, there are the dentists and opticians, hairdressers and florists, and all the other species that are here not only due to the professional prospects, but also because Berlin offers an incomparable "entertainment factor" which practically no one fails to enjoy to the full. Moreover, the horror has enormous effects. Anyone "lucky" enough to be at the right place at the right time, near one of the watch towers dotted along the Wall, may be able to witness an escape bid from "the other side", an attempt that may be successful or may end violently (no, of course no one really wants this to happen; that fact is that this is simply something that may happen unexpectedly, unlooked-for. The reward for such thoughts is a pleasant feeling of nervous tension).

15 September 1965
Youth wants a Satisfaction riot
at the stadium

Even before the British rock band takes to the stage, many amongst the 21,000- strong crowd are already thinking about trouble. Fires will be started and rockets set off. Helmeted riot troops and police are overwhelmed by the mass hysteria that suddenly erupts. And outside, at the stadium doors, many fans unable to get tickets try to force their way in to this open-air concert.

The first Berlin show by UK rock band The Rolling Stones, so long awaited, is the scene of serious incidents. More than 80 people, including 26 police officers, are injured in the riots, and around 90 fans are temporarily detained. The damage to the open-air theatre near the Olympic stadium runs to nearly half a million Marks.

"Sympathy for the Devil" Along with The Beatles, considered "too soft" by many young rebels, The Rolling Stones are ranked as the best rock band in the world.

Concert given by The Rolling Stones at the Berlin stadium. After fans riot, more than 80 people are injured and enormous material damage is caused. In the photograph, an injured fan is stretchered away by ambulance staff.

Wearing scandalously tight trousers, making lascivious androgynous movements and obscene gestures, screaming loudly, with their tenderness and their brutal lyrical attacks, their virtuoso guitar and drum solos, their magnetic stage presence and enviable independence sneering detachment from the rest of the world, The Rolling Stones personify their Berlin fans' hopes and dreams. Hysteria takes over to such an extent that the concert has to be halted after just a couple of songs. Fresh incidents break out at nearby Hallensee station. Seventeen local trains are destroyed in the riot.

The children's anger...
will change the Federal Republic of Germany

Everything is fine. At least, that is what the comfortable, sleepy, conservative section of the population in West Berlin believes. These are the people who went through the Second World War as adults and for whom the order they learned in pre-war days, marked by the mentality passed down from the period of Emperor Wilhelm's reign, continues to be more important than dignity, individuality or self-criticism.

The events that, starting on 5 February 1966, will finally pull to pieces Berlin's self-portrait, already becoming badly cracked, shaking up and eventually changing the entire nation, are discussed by Berliners in an odd mixture of amazed stupor and imperturbable conformism: the intellectual war between civil society and the "intelligentsia" is not a German phenomenon. These generational clashes occur the whole world over.

But in other countries, these potential conflicts, where they broke out, were caused, and their fires fanned, by real, terrible social crises. In the United States, by a decade's involvement, with considerable loss of life, on the part of a country which – or so they believed – was profoundly pacifist, in intrigues in the Far East. In Britain, due to the constant, inglorious loss of what was once one of the world's most powerful empires. In France, caused by the rapid technification (and Americanisation) of a nation deeply reverent towards its traditions. But what on earth was happening in the Federal Republic, particularly in Berlin? In this frontier city whose inhabitants can only feel safe thanks to the fact that the Americans, the British and the French have been warding off the Soviets from them for years?

Since 1945, that is to say, since the time that the seeds of what is now the rebellious "intelligentsia" began to be sown, the Federal Republic – and, above all, Berlin – had enjoyed constant, uninterrupted development, progress, peace, relief and a process of humanisation in private life as an organic growth from inside outward. During this period, the Federal Republic – and Berlin in particular – had suffered no asphyxiating crises, no war, no wave of unemployment, no hunger, no assassination of presidents, no race war, no class justice.

Holidays were longer, women's skirts shorter, cars faster, wages higher and working hours shorter. And, meanwhile, books were becoming "wilder", films more sexist, the weekly magazine *Der Spiegel* ever more sarcastic, students ever more revolutionary, hippies more addicted to drugs. Young people perpetrated ever

The children's anger...

more violent verbal attacks on their elders. So, what on earth was happening here, in Berlin, in the 1960s?

The German Federal Republic –and with it Berlin– is supposed to be the only country in the world that does not need a social crisis in order to explode or implode intellectually. This is, at least, more or less what we understand from the "worthy" conservatism wielded as defensive shield and satirised in *Biedermann & Brandstifter* (a play by Max Frisch known in English as *The Fireraisers*). The flames of conflict are fanned as the old conservatives refuse to listen to the arguments put forward by the young rebels.

5 February 1966
West Berlin students demonstrate against US policy in Vietnam

Around one thousand people take part in a march protesting against US intervention in Vietnam. After the demonstration, around 200 people, mostly students, make for the Amerika Haus in Hardenbergstraße, near Zoo Station. After a sit-down protest has taken place, one group begins throwing paint cans at the building. The police form a protective cordon around the whole block and break up the demonstration.

Vietnam: demonstration in Hardenbergstraße, West Berlin. Behind the poster expressing solidarity with pacifists in the USA are Ekkehard Krippendorf (in the beret) and the famous cabaret artist Wolfgang Neuss (second from the left).

March-April 1966

The communards form Commune 1

In an intolerable act of provocation, young people, men and women, have joined together to form Commune 1. These bourgeois children have actually done that which, when they were only prodigal sons and daughters, they had been content only to dream of. It seems that they neither wash nor brush their hair, they drop their cigarette ends onto the kitchen floor, they wear second-hand clothes, they engage in group sex and smoke hashish. They do this in public, and seem gleefully happy to do so.

Commune I:
Live as you want and show
what you have.

It all happens in an old house with "six and a half bedrooms" on Charlottenburger Kaiser-Friedrich-Straße. Amongst the commune members, who call themselves communards, are Rainer Langhans, Fritz Teufel and Dieter Kunzelmann. The communards, mostly students, pursue alternate lifestyles and behaviour forms. They believe in free love, complete equality of rights between men and women, anti-authoritarian education for children and a complete break with all social rules.

11 December 1966

The confrontation becomes ever more violent

In another violent demonstration against US policy in Vietnam, the State authorities are challenged once more. Outside the Federal Palace in the Bundesallee, the police break up a demonstration when marchers leave the authorised route. At the closing event in the Wittenbergplatz, riot police bring their batons to bear to break up the unruly crowd.

2 June 1967

The day that changed Germany

Persian secret service agents brutally assisting the Berlin police.

It is a warm day in early summer, around eight o'clock in the evening. Several hundred demonstrators march peacefully along Bismarckstraße. The young people, mostly students, shout out the names of bars. Tonight it is time to go out. The Shah of Persia has just gone into the Deutsche Oper opera house by a side entrance to cries of "murderer, murderer". It is a time to be brave in West Berlin. The senator in charge of the police force (by the name of Prill) had already made it clear what would happen if the students took to the streets to demonstrate: "they'll get a baton in the head. This is a good field training for our police officers". Unexpectedly, however, the police are content to shepherd the shah's opponents along a line three metres wide between some construction works and the barriers set up along the public way. Only members of the hated Persian secret service are allowed for a few minutes to operate freely against the demonstrators, with the express authorisation of the head of the police. Meanwhile, the Iranian national anthem is played in the Opera House.

Outside, the students run towards the small gaps on either side of the barriers. A dozen or more ambulances are on hand. At nine minutes past eight in the evening, the police attack the centre of the line which has been blocked off, and start to beat all and sundry. A young man lies, stunned and bleeding on the ground when an officer shouts: "He's just pretending! Give him a bit more then we'll take him away!"

The children's anger...

Once the intervention has been successfully completed, the operation known to the police by the code name "fox hunt" begins. Plainclothed officers, shoulder to shoulder with Persian secret service agents and even Senate drivers patrol streets all around the neighbourhood, hunting down anyone who looks like a student.

The forces of order could hardly be more worked up. Over the loudspeakers they have heard the false rumour that demonstrators have stabbed a police officer to death. Moreover, this is the first time that they have seen students resisting the public authorities. Several attempts are made to free those arrested.

Karl-Heinz Karras, head of the political police criminal brigade, is surrounded after a group of demonstrators has been arrested. Karras pulls out his pistol and takes the safety catch off. Other uniformed officers run to assist him. They chase after a demonstrator who flees in panic after seeing the man take out his gun, and this, combined with his red shirt and unruly conduct, serves only to inflame their spirits more. Catching up with the boy, they tackle him, bringing him crashing to the ground. Karras, the criminal brigade officer, holds his pistol in his hand, the safety catch still off. A shot rings out, the bullet going straight into the head of the cornered demonstrator.

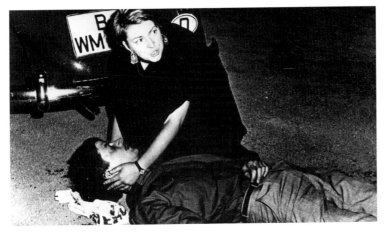

... West Berlin politics – and the city's police – have lost their innocence.

The student Benno Ohnesorg lies bleeding, mortally wounded by Karl-Heinz Karras, head of the criminal brigade, in the arms of a passer-by, Friederike Hausmann (or Dollinger).

Benno Ohnesorg, 26 years old, a university student majoring in Romance languages and literature, a pacifist and a practising Christian, died from gunshot wounds shortly after being taken to hospital. That night, calm reigns at the meeting points of the Berlin left-wing scene around the Kurfürstendamm. The record players have been turned off. An end has come, too, to the meetings enlivened by beer, a long-standing tradition in which Berlin's anarchic bohemia engaged in heated debates with worthy representatives of the bourgeoisie.

The children's anger...

The days, weeks and months following the scandal that rocked the State

Still nothing has been achieved. To the point where there are absolutely no grounds for optimism, as the agitated students are to learn the next morning when the radio broadcasts an announcement by Heinrich Albertz, a clergyman, social democrat and mayor: "The State has reached the end of its patience", Albertz announces. The demonstrators can claim "the sad merit, not only of insulting a guest of the Federal Republic of Germany, but also of causing a death and injuries to many."
That same day, fast-track court cases are held and a general (and illegal) prohibition against all demonstrations is put into effect.

To the postwar generation, it is not only the dark suits of their university professors and the antiquated legal eagles that smell bad. The affair also gives off the whiff of Nazi double stands, blind belief in superiority, the myth of the war and the defeat and the authoritarian ways in which their fathers had been educated in all this. The spirit of this generation, which dominates in all walks of life, appears invulnerable: 70% of high executives over 50 years of age are from elite groups in the Third Reich. Those that dare to oppose them are scornfully labelled as "communists" or "drop-outs." The older generation regard and treat as scum all men they meet on the streets with long hair, a friendly look and tight trousers, quickly judging them on looks alone. And the threat – though there is no substance behind it – of "work camps" is heard once more here, in Berlin.
The media warn of a revolution on the way. And they give this danger a name: Rudi Dutschke. In 1967, Dutschke has everything that the "citizens' terror" should have, and he is described in the press as the figurehead of youth rebellion.

Faith in human goodness: Dutschke with his wife and child.

Despite this erroneous description, one given wide credence nonetheless, Dutschke was not the German Che Guevara; rather, he was a Don Quixotte who waged a non-violent war against the windmills of fascist world imperialism. An incorruptible ascetic who believed in God, in the natural goodness of people and in a fair and just society, Dutschke devoured revolutionary literature and marched at the head of demonstrations with his pockets full of books. For a while, he even began to believe what his enemies said about him: that he was a "revolutionary". If these inter-generational skirmishes had not served to reveal the German people's deathly severity, the civil war that was enacted in West Berlin would have been more of an operetta than a tragedy. (In 2005, after Dutschke had suffered defamation lasting many years and long after his death, caused by the injuries he received in the brutal attack, the city of Berlin named a street after this civil rights leader. The need he had proclaimed of non-violently infiltrating bourgeois institutions by taking up state government posts was gradually fulfilled.)

Very few people finally open their eyes to reality and call for moderation after the events of 2 June 1967. These few do, however, include the person politically responsible for the massacre outside the Opera House: Heinrich Albertz. Confessing that "the weaker I was, the harder I negotiated", Albertz resigned as mayor. Those who speak with him over this period see a man horrified at himself. A man who finds it impossible now to understand how blindness and opportunistic hunger for power had undermined his reason and conscience.

His successor, Klaus Schütz, a former frontier guard even more arrogant than Albertz, is free from such scruples. Supported by many sympathisers and various newspapers, Schütz not only orchestrates the "campaign against the students", indeed he raises it to a man-hunt on the level of the pogrom. It is possible to identify students who are enemies of the state just by looking at them, he assures "decent" Berliners. "You have to look at these types. You have to look them right in the face." That they can in some way be expelled, that this rebellious generation can be simply got rid off, is what the city's mayor means when he says, in public: "If necessary, I can do without the students." His heart in his hand, Schütz speaks to those whose work has enabled West Berlin "to rise again" and who do not want to see their ideas about the world dragged through the mud. "Work camps" and "concentration camps"; that is what working Berliners want for the demonstrators they point their fingers at, but also other, more terrible things. As the magazine *Stern* reports at this time (a period lasting weeks and months), the slogan "Gas Rudi Dutschke" has appeared on the walls of many buildings.

A desperate student screams out to his comrades at this time: "You cannot talk to them! They are the Auschwitz generation!" The student, whose name is Gudrun Enslin, will later go on to found the Red Army Faction (Rote Armee Fraktion), or RAF, also known as the Baader-Meinhof Gang.

"...the weaker I was, the harder I negotiated".

Heinrich Albertz, mayor of Berlin.

17-18 February 1968
The student revolt reaches boiling point

On June 17, at the Maximum Auditorium in the Technical University, the "International Congress on Vietnam" begins. The even, organised by left-wing student groups, brings together some three thousand participants to criticise the USA under a huge Vietcong flag, announcing the imminent victory of the "Vietnamese revolution".

The children's anger...

In a brilliant speech, Rudi Dutschke, the main theoretician behind the German Socialist Students Federation (Sozialistischen Deutschen Studentenbund or SDS) calls for "anti-imperialist struggle in the great cities."

The next day, twelve thousand sympathisers carrying posters of Lenin and Ho Chi Minh march down the Kurfürstendamm in central West Berlin in a demonstration called by the congress.

Ordinary people attack demonstrating students: "To the concentration camp!"

11 April 1968
Rudi Dutschke is shot

By early 1968, the student revolt that started in Berlin had reached most of the principal university cities in West Germany. The generation clash always follows the West Berlin model, though not always with the same hysterical brutality. Until, in Berlin, a worker shoots down the symbol of student protest in the Kurfürstendamm.

(Rudi Dutschke, 28 years of age, is shot and wounded by several bullets from a revolver in the Kurfürstendamm at the point where it meets Joachim-Friedrich-Straße. The injuries he suffers include a bullet to the brain, for which he is operated on for several hours at the Westend Hospital. Years later, he was to die partly from the lasting effects caused by these wounds).

Soon after the shooting, the police track down the person responsible, a 23-year-old house painter, Josef Bachmann, from Peine, in the cellar of a house near the Nestorstraße. Bachmann attempts to resist arrest and is slightly wounded in the shooting that results. From the police questioning, it becomes clear that the young house painter believed what he read in the newspapers, and that by killing Rudi Dutschke he was becoming a heroic saviour for

The children's anger...

Shooting of Rudi Dutschke, leader of the German Socialist Students Federation (SDS), in the Kurfürstendamm, Berlin: police around the crime scene, marked by chalk.

"decent" Germany. News of the attack quickly spreads all over Federal Germany and serious incidents break out, particularly in Berlin, as students and opposition leaders demonstrate outside the parliament (APO). As police struggle to contain the demonstrators, news of two more deaths in Munich comes through: a student and a news photographer have been killed during riots sparked off by protests against the shooting of Rudi Dutschke. The West Berlin police take rigorous measures in the most orderly manner. The Berlin population is in a state of shock. More than two thousand demonstrators are bearing down from the Technical University to the headquarters of publishing group Springer in Kreuzberger Kochstraße. They consider Springer the intellectual instigator of the attack on Dutschke due to the defamatory newspaper campaign it has orchestrated (this is an opinion that, years later, the German political authorities will finally accept as correct).

Like civil war: Batons and water cannon, used against demonstrators protesting in Berlin against the attack on Rudi Dutschke.

The children's anger...

In riots around the Springer headquarters, windows are smashed and company transport vehicles are set on fire using Molotov cocktails.

Fierce battles take place over the following days. At the centre of events are the Springer publishing group and, once more, the Kurfürstendamm. Here, on the corner with Uhlandstraße, demonstrators stop the traffic, whilst the police finally clear the area with a baton charge. The publishing company building is closed off by barbed wire fences and hundreds of police. On Easter Monday, April 16, university professors stage a demonstration in the Hammarskjöldplatz the Charlottenburg under the slogan "Start Again". This demo, which draws thousands of students, goes off peacefully. Dutschke's supporters defend their goal of mobilising minorities inside and outside the universities against the despised system imposed by the governing classes. For days and weeks, rebellious young people orchestrate moves aimed at one sole aim: that of infiltrating the establishment – teaching staff and places of power – using peaceful means.

Change begins in the Federal Republic of Germany

The revolutionaries of those days have since become judges and prosecutors. Just like the former streetfighter and current minister for foreign affairs, Joschka Fischer, they have made their career in politics or occupy posts as teachers and professors at faculties and universities. It is they who have changed or repealed laws, they who have put reform in motion. Education has changed: this is, without doubt, one of the most important steps towards installing a free, democratic society formed by truly emancipated citizens. Moves towards equal rights for men and women are made, and understanding for other cultures spreads, with greater tolerance extended towards the more heterodox members of society. As a result of the youth revolution, West Germany undergoes a kind of silent cultural revolution, one that is accepted and even wished, since more and more as a natural process.

The danger represented by those excluded

The most extremist ultra-leftists withdraw, dissatisfied. They have achieved very few of their goals. The "post-fascist" morality of the "stinking" 50s and 60s has been smashed to pieces but, thanks to this, the structures of the democratic, capitalist state have merely been reinforced. After undergoing an anxious period of crisis, the Federal Republic has become a western democracy almost without a struggle, with a generation of willing young people committed and sure of themselves and what they are doing. Outside these circles, little had been heard about the "infiltration" that Dutschke preached and was proposed by the more moderate left. The harvest of the seeds sown by Dutschke had yet to be reaped.

The extreme left was sceptical about the situation. Members of these groups refused to believe in the gradual dissolution of the dominant structures put in place by their "elders", but neither did they try hard to believe in such a thing.

Towards the end of the 1960s, the most extreme core of left-wing extremists formed the Red Army Faction (RAF), the most dangerous active terrorist group in the Federal Republic of Germany. Also known as the Baader-Meinhof Gang, the RAF had links to several clandestine movements abroad, using their training camps to prepare their own members for the struggle ahead.

14 May 1970
RAF terrorist Andreas Baader freed by masked gang

Andreas Baader, who lived in Berlin in the early 1960s, a petty criminal sentenced in 1968 to three years in prison in Frankfurt for starting a fire in a department store, is freed in Berlin by a group of fellow terrorists. Baader, who was serving his time at Berlin's Tegel penitentiary, had obtained permission from the prison authorities to study works at the Deutsches Zentralinstitut für soziale Fragen in Dahlem. It appears he was working with his tutor, Ulrike Meinhof, on a book about juvenile delinquency.

He began his "career" as a petty criminal in Berlin: Andreas Baader in 1970.

The attack on the Deutsches Zentralinstitut leads to shooting between the masked accomplices attempting to free Baader and the two law enforcement officers charged with minding the RAF leader. A 62-year-old worker at the research institute is seriously wounded, shot by several bullets. Ulrike Meinhof and the other two people involved in the breakout manage to escape with Baader through a window, disappearing into underground life in Berlin.

27 February 1975
RAF kidnaps a Berlin political leader

Peter Lorenz, Berlin regional president of the Christian Democrat Union and his party's candidate at the imminent mayoral elections, is kidnapped by RAF terrorists.

At nine in the morning, the 53-year-old lawyer and notary public is being driven by his chauffeur to his office when his official car

The children's anger...

is blocked by a lorry in Quermatenweg (Zehlendorf). Three people alight from the lorry and, after a brief scuffle, in which the chauffeur is beaten, the two men and a woman hustle Lorenz into a waiting car and drive off with him.

The next day, allied terrorist group Movement 2 June (name in memory of the day that Benno Ohnesorg was shot by a policeman) sends the press of photograph of Lorenz in captivity and demand that six comrades should be freed and an aeroplane provided, ready to fly them abroad. In order to save the life of the CDU politician, the crisis committee hastily set up gives in to these demands. On March 4, as a guarantee that the terrorists' conditions will be met, Heinz Albertz, former president and mayor of Berlin, flies to Aden with the freed prisoners. On March 5, Lorenz himself is freed.

Peter Lorenz.

Captured by the Movement June 2 terrorist group.

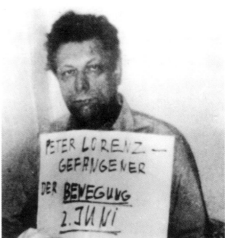

February 1976
Brrrr...! The Berlinale puts on its woolly hat

At previous festivals, which took place in June each year, the stuff of dreams had been displayed in the streets. From now on, the annual Berlinale will take place in February, however, as from an organisational standpoint the summer date is uncomfortably close to that of the Venice Biennial. Moreover, the event is turned into more of an event for hardened film fans. "Normal" Berliners are terribly disappointed. However, the content has also changed somewhat. Intellectual concerns and needs now predominate over previous years' cult for famous stars, combined with a certain intellectual hoo-hah and a sensationalist satisfaction in lavish expenditure. The new format and philosophy may be less popular amongst "the man in the street", but it will be justified by attracting the most outstanding directors to bring their ambitious productions to Berlin.

10 October 1978

West Berlin: drug Mecca

Whether they are rockers, beatniks, soul fans or psychedelic hippies, drugs – above all alcohol and amphetamines – play an important role in all youth cultures and so-called marginal or underground groups. Drugs formed part of their life, though they were not considered an important issue. They did begin to cause concern, however, when, along with hashish and marihuana, a material emerged in industrialised countries in the west that was, moreover, illegal, an aspect that considerably increased its power of attraction.

In just a short time, these narcotics became a drug used massively by a complex international pop culture that was intimately linked to world protest movements. No one with ears to hear could fail to notice the countless allusions to drugs in British and American pop culture. *Everybody Must Get Stoned*, ordered Bob Dylan, whilst Pink Floyd and Jimi Hendrix, the Rolling Stones and The Beatles played the soundtrack to the LSD trip, laced with oriental sounds.

The general public was bemused. What was happening before their very eyes, at beat clubs, in tea parlours and at concerts, could only end, as a leaflet distributed by Berlin criminal police made clear, "in prison, in a reformatory or in the mental hospital".

The more absurd were certain arguments in favour of prohibition, the more insolent young people were towards the moral double standards of decent preachers against drugs who nevertheless were quite happy to consume alcohol and the quicker the desire to mount a provocative opposition to such moves grew. And never before had the pharmaceutical industry launched on the market over such a short period of time so many psychoactive substances as in the 1960s. This was the decade of the psycho pills: Valium, Librium, Nobrium, Captagon, Prellodin, AN 1...

The simplicity of those Flower Power days had arrived on the scene accompanied by "sister morphine" and cocaine. Now times were becoming harder, and so were drugs. LSD and heroin were taking over.

Staggering along the pavement and holding themselves up against the walls, their eyes vacant, just waiting for hours, waiting for someone to come along, someone to whom their unfortunate appearance will cause that special "click" that will persuade them to help fund their habit, their addiction, enabling them to

A complete wreck: a heroin addict.

Ever younger victims are falling into the mire of Berlin's drug culture. Christiane F., portrayed in We Children From The Zoo Station, was a child heroin addict.

The children's anger...

give themselves up to it body and soul... Christiane F., 16 years old, was, in 1978, one of approximately ten thousand heroin addicts in Berlin. She had first tried "soft" drugs at the local church youth club when she was 12, and at 13 tried heroin at a discotheque, quickly becoming hooked. She experienced pain and saw death as a member of a gang of young junkies. In the morning she went to school and in the afternoon she worked as a prostitute in the infamous Bahnhof Zoo area. For nearly two years, she managed to hide her addiction from her mother.
The heroin trade had absolute control over schools, discotheques and youth clubs. The story of Christiane F., entitled *We Children From The Zoo Station*, became a best seller rivalled only by the likes of Snow White and Winnetou.

31 December 1980
More than 10% of immigrants in Germany live in Berlin

Numbers of foreign immigrants living in Berlin also rises sharply in 1980. There are now approximately 230,000 foreigners living in the city, that is to say, that one in nine "Berliners" holds a nationality other than German. Compared to federal territory, where foreign workers began to be taken on in the early-1950s, Berlin's foreign workforce had been relatively unimportant economically until the construction of the Wall (1961).
In 1961, foreign residents, a total of around 22,500 people, represented 1% of the entire West Berlin population. This later recruitment of foreign workers led to a peculiar make-up of specific nationalities on the "island", with above-average numbers of Turks (50%) and Yugoslavs (14%). By this time, reserves of workers from the traditional suppliers (Italy, Spain and Greece) were pretty much exhausted.

22 September 1981
Deaths in riots against property speculators

During violent confrontations between demonstrators and police, 18-year-old Klaus-Jürgen Rattey is knocked down by a bus in Potsdamer street on the corner with Bülowstraße in Schöneberg, later dying from his injuries. Rattey belonged to a rather violent group of demonstrators protesting against the eviction of squatters from eight houses that they had occupied, ordered by the Senate.
When news of the young man's death begins to spread, rioting breaks out, particularly in Schöneberg, practically a civil war that

lasts until well into the night. More than one hundred people are injured in these violent incidents. Demonstrators and by-standers blame the police in part for the mortal accident: it appears that riot police had pushed Rattey's group back towards the busy crossroads. The police deny this version of events. According to information released by the Senate, there are 152 squats in the city. By June, however, the number of houses illegally occupied has risen to reach its highest point: 165.

Graffiti on the walls protesting about the many vacant houses in the city.

20 January 1984
GDR refugees refuse to leave the US Embassy

Whilst border fortifications are perfected in East Berlin and the Wall is doubled in width around the Brandenburg Gate, six GDR citizens apply for political asylum in the US Embassy in East Berlin, refusing to leave the building peacefully.

In letters to the US president, Ronald Reagan, and to the president of the Council of State, Erich Honecker, the six insist in their demand to leave the GDR. After intense negotiations over two days, the refugees are given permission to exit the country. On January 22, they cross from East to West Berlin at the Invalidenstraße checkpoint, accompanied by a high official from the Federal Republic of Germany.

(In June 1984, a total of 55 GDR citizens manage to get into the Federal Republic of Germany's permanent delegation in East Berlin. On June 27, visits are temporarily ended. The refugees gradually begin to leave the West German delegation on June 27, several after taking refuge there for months).

31 December 1985

Berlin, Germany's leading destination, is also a unique culinary paradise

In 1985, West Berlin's 4,785 restaurants report annual income of 1,220 million marks, providing jobs for 20,000 people. These figures make Berlin the German city with the most restaurant establishments. Apart from the many eateries serving Berlin and German cuisine (including specialities from other states forming part of the federation), there are more than Italian 800 restaurants, 300 Yugoslavian and around 100 Asian establishments. Berlin is now Europe's third most popular tourist destination, after London and Paris. The main attraction of West Berlin is that here, unlike cities in the rest of Germany and much of Europe, there are no closing times. Apart from a short break for cleaning, bars, restaurants and clubs can stay open 24 hours a day.
(In 1991, shortly after German reunification, Berlin boasted more than 6,000 bars, discotheques and nightclubs, cafés and restaurants. Of these, 4,600 are in West Berlin and 1,400 in East Berlin).

The Wall begins to shake

25 November 1987
The Church protects opposition groups

The nerves of the GDR regime are beginning to crack. Throughout 1987, confrontations in East Berlin between the state powers and opposition groups have escalated dangerously. The State Security Service (Stasi) and People's Police are ever more brutal as they work hand-in-hand with the justice system to repress pacifist and environmentalist groups as they work hand-in-hand with the justice system.

Today, 25 November 1987, the police stormed a building adjoining the Zionskirche in Prenzlauer Berg containing an environmental library and arrested several members of ecologist and human rights groups. The state prosecutor's office confirms that those arrested in the building were caught "red-handed, writing hostile articles against the State." Growing numbers of East Berliners are beginning to rebel against these constant, repeated and ever more exacerbated repressive measures.

Today, too, at a spontaneously-organised protest demonstration, hundreds of citizens have demanded the immediate release of the prisoners. Leaders of the Berlin-Brandenburg Evangelical Church also join the protest, stressing that the Church opposes all State attempts at intimidation and that it will try to protect any seriously threatened member of opposition groups.

17 January 1988
Blows exchanged at commemoration for Rosa Luxemburg

During the "battle demonstration" which takes place each January 17 to mark the assassinations of Rosa Luxemburg and Karl Liebknecht, an open exchange of blows occurred between opponents of the regime and the police. More than 150 members of pacifist and human rights groups joined the demonstration, attended by more than 200,000 people, mostly SED officials, marching to Rosa Luxembourg's grave in Friedrichsfelde. When a banner stating that "Freedom is always freedom for dissenters" Stasi members mixing with demonstrators hurl themselves at the protestors. Fighting breaks out,

The Wall begins to shake

at the end of which 120 people are arrested. Those detained by the Stasi also include Stephan Krawzyk, a singer-songwriter forbidden from performing, and his wife, film director Freya Klier.

7 May 1989

Angry protests at electoral fraud

The municipal district meeting that takes place on this day goes off in exactly the way opponents of the regime feared. According to official figures, 98.63% of the population has voted for the single list of candidates presented by the National Front. Even for SED officials, this is a truly surprising confirmation of support for GDR domestic policy. In view of growing citizen discontent with circumstances in the GDR, doubts about the results are made public. The authorities are accused of lying about the election results. Civil rights groups that observed the vote count in several districts openly talk of State-sponsored electoral fraud. State security forces break up the spontaneous demonstration in Alexanderplatz almost as soon as it starts.

6 October 1989

Hopes placed in Gorbachev

Despite the explosive political situation in the country, the government decides to throw a party for itself to mark the 40th anniversary of the GDR. Mijail Gorbachev, in whom many East Berliners have deposited their hopes, is invited to attend the ceremony, which will revolve around a large programme of activities.

"Life punishes those who come too late."

Erich Honecker welcomes PCUS general secretary Mijail Gorbachev on his arrival in East Berlin.

Gorbachev, who first launched political reform in the Soviet Union, is well-placed – or at least that is what many hope – to persuade the GDR government of the need to change its political line. And then came the quote with which the Soviet leader dumbfounded his host and breathed hope into opponents of the regime. To a question posed by a journalist as to whether the GDR should undergo reform, he answered: "Life punishes those who come too late."

4 November 1989

Largest protest demonstration Government faced by capitulation

Demonstration calling for reform in the GDR, called by various organisations and groups of artists, attended by nearly 750,000 people.

Free press for free men! Don't let them use you!

This is the day when the moment of "change" comes for most East Berliners. Today, something no GDR citizen believed possible actually occurs. In the Alexanderplatz, the people rise up in the largest mass demonstration that has taken place in the entire history of the GDR. During the workers' rising in 1953, it was the workers who bravely made their way to the front, those who said: People have to run some risks and they have to know how to live with this. But, above all, they need to want it when they know what their goal is. At that moment, only the workers could see things clearly: no one who wants to move on can ever keep both feet on the ground. They have to take some risks! The expansive wave of uprising burst forth, and the "drops" could be seen: the pain for each of the victims moved family members, friends and everyone else who suffered with them. Those in power covered the rebellions in despicable clichés and calumny.

But here, today, 36 years, 4 months and a few days later, even average citizens are prepared to take their feet from the ground they stand on. More than half a million people assemble at the "Alex". The writers Christa Wolf and Stefan Heym (after the fall of the Wall, would become chairman of the Federal Parliament by virtue of being its oldest member) addressed the crowd in speeches that, relayed by loudspeakers, said what, until now, millions of people all over the GDR had only dared to think. But the State powers had not yet given up. Whilst accepting that it was impossible to respond violently to such a large gathering, the regime attempts to use its propagandists to bring the situation under control. Representatives from the government take the stand, pick up the microphone... Günther Schabowski, SED head for Berlin, and Markus Wolf, former GDR chief of espionage services, try to speak, but are interrupted and booed by the crowd.

The game is over. The cards are re-shuffled

The 40 years that the GDR existed will go down in German history as four decades of tyranny, terror and propaganda, a State structure that was only held together by a carrot tied to a stick, an experiment that resulted in an abysmal failure. The only really outstanding peculiarity that will remain in the memory will be the image of human beings profoundly miserable.)

The note that will change universal history

"With immediate effect!"

Günter Schabowski announces that the border is to open at a press conference broadcast live on television.

9 November 1989
Was opening the border a "mistake"?

The events that take place in Berlin this afternoon and evening and throughout the following night will keep the whole world on tenterhooks: Günter Schabowski, member of the SED politburo, will drop the bombshell in apparent calm during an international press conference broadcast live, with the statement that the GDR government has decided to lift the rules governing travelling abroad, "effectively leaving the Republic". The entire world can see the note that Schabowski is holding in his hand, and from which he reads out the new decree regulating entries and exits from the country, approved by the council of ministers. GDR citizens can request permission for private travel into foreign countries without the conditions that have held until now. Permission will be granted instantly. "When will this enter into force?" asks a journalist. Schabowski glances at his paper and replies: "from this moment on, immediately!"

The note that will change universal history

The news spreads like wildfire. All over the city, in houses, on the underground, on local trains, on buses, in the street, everybody is asking each other: "Have you heard? They say the borders are open."

Before ten o'clock that even, the first crowds of East Berliners have assembled to force the first mass release. However, those manning the checkpoints have not been informed about any of this. In view of the avalanche that wants to cross the border in Bornholmer Straße, at around 11.15 a captain of the border guard decides to negotiate on his own initiative. After repeated requests for information have been ignored, he feels that his own superiors have abandoned him and decides to open up the border under his own responsibility. Similar scenes are happening at the other checkpoints in Berlin. Six hours later, all official border checkpoints in the city are open. Thousands of joyful Berliners assemble around the wall at the Brandenburg Gate. All television and radio stations are broadcasting events life. That night, convoys of *trabbis* and *wartburgs* make for the Kurfürstendamm, horns blaring. East Berliners, awoken from their long sleep, hug sisters, brothers, parents, children, friends, strangers, laughing, crying, trembling with emotion. They embrace and kiss effusively, shaken and excited by recent events.

Berlin celebrates its own reunification until the early hours. On the Mövenpick pavement café in the Europa-Center, opposite the Gedächtniskirche church and in countless cafeterias and bars, champagne glasses clink together. "This is completely crazy", is the phrase repeated everywhere. "Crazy", that is the word most used on this night, when people can hardly speak for their joy. Even the most cynical find they have a frog in their throats, even the toughest guys have to fight back the tears.

"Crazy!"
Joyful Berliners.

On the night from 9 to 10 November 1989, East Berliners climb the Wall at the Brandenburg Gate.

The note that will change universal history

The politburo, caught in complete disarray

A very different atmosphere reigns at SED politburo headquarters in the early hours of this historic night. The powers that be rack their brains to see how this state of affairs has come about. "Who has played this trick on us?" asks Honecker's successor Egon Krenz, disconcerted as he seeks someone to blame (before, like Schabowski, claiming the "heroic" act of opening up as his own decision).

The new government calls for calm.

Berlin SED organisation members appear before the central committee to call for reformation of the party: secretary general Egon Krenz and politburo member Günter Schabowski attempt to calm demonstrators.

Was the announcement that foreign travel conditions were to be lifted, made at a press conference broadcast live on television, a simple mistake, a mere error of interpretation? Countless legends spring up over the days and weeks following that unforgettable 9 November 1989. What is true, at least, is that the note whose contents Schabowski had let slip was a document from the GDR council of ministers which Schabowski had read out without mistake.

("We never dreamt that opening the Wall meant the beginning of the end for the GDR. On the contrary, we hoped to bring about a gradual stabilisation process", says Günter Schabowski, designated by Egon Krenz to represent the SED politburo at future press conferences).

The new GDR government, led by Egon Krenz, did not intend the borders to be opened in this way. What they hoped for was to gradually lift conditions on foreign travel. That was the decision the politburo had taken. They had to admit that East Berlin was like a pressure cooker about to explode, and that they needed to let some steam out immediately, though very carefully and little

30 June 1990

At midnight, Hagen Koch, the GDR special delegate for the conservation of the wall (photographed here) hands over the historic Checkpoint Charlie Rainer Hildebrandt, founder and director of the Berlin Wall Museum.

by little to ensure that the contents did not spill out completely. But their blinkered adherence to ideology meant that the East German leaders failed to understand that the human seas they had unleashed would bring the Wall down and that nothing could now hold the contents of the "pot" in, and that nothing would ever return to that pot.

(Not only the world of the victims had been torn down, but also that of its creators, and even the world of former politburo members Egon Krenz and Siegfried Lorenz. Years after the fall of the Wall, in February 2005, they had still not got over their shock at what they had lost. As members of the party set up to replace the SED, the PDS, both made no bones in boasting about their authoritarian past in the new communist party's grassroots newsletter. Both also accused the Soviet reformer Mikhail Gorbachev of treachery. "Behind the back of the GDR government" they write, the path towards Germany reunification was paved "as if we had never been allies." And both know that they are being misleading when they reach the conclusion that, had it not been for this treachery, the GDR would still exist today, even though, in their opinion, "we know that there has been an international conspiracy against socialism").

10 November 1989
West Berlin surprised and still hesitant

On this day, the West Berlin chamber of representatives approves a resolution on the present situation in the GDR. At this time, the SED having been dissolved, it is possible to hope for reunification of the two German states, but not yet to believe in it: "We support the desire for freedom to travel", declares the chamber in comments on recent events, "and the demand for free elections and an end to one party's monopoly of power. We call on the GDR government to open up the way towards immediate, free, general elections by secret ballot."

8 December 1989
The SED adopts the PDS disguise

Radical change is going ahead at a dizzying speed. On November 13, the East Berlin people's chamber elects Hans Modrow, considered to be part of the reformist current within the SED, as president of the GDR council of ministers. This is followed on December 3 by the resignation of Egon Krenz, party leader and chief of state.

Today, December 8, the SED holds a special assembly at the Dynamo sports hall at which Gregor Gysi, a lawyer (and former defender of critics of the regime facing trial) is elected president. (Thanks to Gysi, a charismatic leader, the PDS is surprisingly successful at the elections that take place in the new federal states over coming years).

At the assembly, delegates also openly criticise the old one-party regime and publish an apology to the German people for the "crisis that endangered the existence of the GDR" and for which they were responsible.

(Soon after this, the public learns that the SED is changing its name in the future to PDS (Party of Democratic Socialism). The next question that arises is why the party does not undergo a process of reformation. The crucial answer to this is not revealed until it is learned that the SED has resources running into hundreds of millions of marks, and that the PDS claims to be the former party's legal heir).

The last exit stamp before the Wall opened.

3 October 1990
Germany is reunified at last

Today is the day of German Reunification. Today, 3 October 1990, the GDR becomes part of the Federal Republic of Germany by agreement of the people's chamber. The division of Berlin and Germany is formerly ended.

(the first all-Berlin parliament freely elected since 1946 is convened on 11 January 1991 at the Nikolaikirche (in Mitte) at a constitutive session. A few days later, the first mayor of all Berlin, the future capital is appointed. The first mayor in this new chapter of Berlin's history is Eberhard Diepgen (CDU), who forms a great coalition with the social democrats).

Trabbis making for West Berlin.

The GDR opens its borders with West Berlin and the whole Federal Republic to its citizens: visitors cross lines of West Berlin schoolchildren as they cross the Böse bridge into the Wedding district.

A whistle-stop journey through time

Collage of images:
The Brandenburg Gate over the centuries.

With the Prussian flag, the swastika, the GDR flag and the present flag, that of the FRG.

The Berlin landscape began to form after the last glacial period. Even now, the basic contours that shape this landscape can be seen under the grid lines of asphalt and concrete: the Spree Valley, which once carried the melting glacial water between the moraine hills behind Barnim, in the North, and what is now Teltow district in the South. In this landscape, covered by typical tundra flora, lived the first known "Berliners", for a few months in the summer during the tenth millennium BC. These small groups of 10-15 reindeer hunters were what we might call "seasonal Berliners". The Ice Age ended here in around 8,000 BC, and the many stone axe heads found show that people settled in the green forests that soon grew as the earth slowly warmed up. This was when sedentary hunting began to flourish here, rather than Nomadic reindeer herds. The menu included moose, deer, roe deer and wild boar. Hunters also became sedentary, supplementing their diet with the fish they caught. However, food obtained from advances in agricultural and livestock farming, discovered long ago in the Far East, did not reach these parts into the second half of the fourth millennium BC. These later "Berliners" would also benefit from another invention, one which would also stimulate their artistic abilities: pottery, useful for cooking and keeping food.

A whistle-stop journey through time

Artist's vision of a German
farm at around the time of
the birth of Christ.

(Bilder zur deutschen
Vorgeschichte recreation
"Images from German
prehistory", 1936)

The Bronze Age began in Germany with the introduction here of bronze in the 18th century BC.

Larger settlements began to become established in this area in the 11th and 10th centuries BC. Around one thousand people, distributed in small villages, lived here as farmers. Iron began to be used in around 700 BC, used at first only to make jewellery. However, the settlement process was slowed down at this time by worsening climate conditions.

Over the coming centuries, population density began to increase once more, reaching its height in the 1st century AD.

Findings of Roman coins and imported products demonstrating the growing increase of the Roman Empire here. With it, a ray of light will illuminate the darkness of this area, unreached as yet by writing systems. Thanks to the Roman historian Cornelius Tacitus, the world can call the inhabitants of the Berlin area by their name: Germanic Senones of the Elba. Both their name and their habitat are found in Tacitus' *Germania*, a work whose revelations about the Germans have been increased by many archaeological finds in and around Berlin, dating to the 1st century AD, and providing decisive confirmation. These excavations have shown that the Senones lived in villages, in farms separated one from another and delimited by valleys. Generally speaking, farms consisted of the main building, some of them up to 30 metres long, including a living area with kitchen, a covered stable and one or two granaries built on pillars to protect them from

A whistle-stop journey through time

rodents. All this was made of wood, with constructions made from posts and filled with esparto grass and mud walls.

Generally speaking, the Senones burnt their dead: Burial was only given to bodies in tombs with many gifts. After incineration, the ashes were kept in clay urns.

In the 3rd century AD, a small Roman statue of Jupiter arrived in the territory, and was placed in a tomb with various burial urns. The influence of Roman art was seen more and more, particularly in portrayals of Jupiter, the most important god and symbol of Rome's power.

The body has been conserved in rather good condition. A farmer's daughter, around 17 years old, unearthed in the Britz district of Berlin, she was buried in 529 AD. Amongst the remains of her tongue, researchers discovered a tiny Christian cross. A sensational find which served to prove that the first Christians became established in this area at a relatively late date. But the young girl had also been given a ten-Pfennig coin to pay for her journey into the netherworld. Christian and pagan are still mixed.

The adoption of Christian practices may also be the reason for which, little by little, the custom of incinerating the dead was replaced by burial, particularly amongst the more well-to-do families. A comb, brooches, a knife and some scissors were also found in the tomb of the young girl. Also – and this is the most important find – a greenish glass bowl from the Mainz area. It is likely that the bowl reached what is now Berlin via Thuringia. The Germans who lived on the banks of the Havel and the Spree traded widely with surrounding tribes.

In around 720, Slav settlers came to this region. They built villages and lived peacefully with what remained of the German population. Even in 1180, the German tribes continued to migrate. They merely passed through the area where Berlin would one day stand.

The German King Otto the Great founded the bishopric of Havelberg and Brandenburg and launched the country's systematic conversion to Christianity. The future Potsdam is first mentioned in the year 993 as "locus Poztupinum", which means "situated on the slopes of the mountain").

In 1150, after many revolts and rebellions, the future Berlin passed into the hands of Albrecht, the Bear, who ruled over Havelland and Brandenburg with a view to the future.

The name Berlin is mentioned for the first time in a church document dated 26 January 1244. There follow registers of the

The Dolichenus Jupiter, a 3rd-century bronze Roman sculpture found in Lichtenberg.

A whistle-stop journey through time

The oldest-known Berlin seal (1235).

The animal depicted is the eagle of the Marquis of Brandenburg.

First mention of Berlin in a document: 26 January 1244

names of a series of villages which will, in the future, form the basis for the districts of Berlin.

Berlin's first fortifications were built in 1247: a circular wall all around the city. Berlin and tiny Cölln (a village corresponding to what is today the huge Neukölln district) are joined by a long bridge.

Soon after obtaining their town charter, Berlin began to expand its territory, establishing new villages. The bear, famous symbol of the city, appeared for the first time on a stamp dated 22 March 1280.

Fifty-three years later, the German King Ludwig of Bavaria claimed the land containing more than a score of cities in Brandenburg province (including Berlin Spandau and Köpenick), which join together in a defensive alliance. In Berlin, a mob storms the provost's house and kills the owner. The Vatican responds by imposing its harshest punishment on Berlin: excommunication.

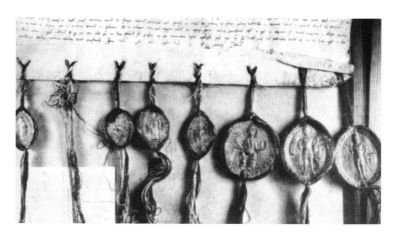

In 1348, the plague that is devastating all Europe also descends on Berlin. One-third of the German population is killed by the Black Death. The Jews are blamed for this catastrophe, and cruelly persecuted. They are said to have poisoned wells and sold food in bad condition.

In 1380, a terrible fire destroys much of the city. A knight whose clan is at war with the cities of the Spree is found guilty of starting the fire, and is put to death. Twenty-one cities join Berlin in a defensive alliance against the hordes of marauding bandits.

In 1446, the Elector Frederick II, known as "Irontooth", imprisons all Jews and confiscates their property.

In 1354, Jews were limited to a marginal place in economic and social affairs, and were only permitted to act as money-lenders and -changers (anonymous woodcut, dated around 1360).

In 1450, the population of Berlin stands at around 8,000. "Irontooth" requires each house to send one "armed soldier" as cannon fodder in his battles against the Saxons.

The Elector rules with an iron fist. He orders a tailor, accused of heresy, to be burned at the stake in the middle of the market place to entertain the people.

On 11 March 1486, Albrecht III, Achilles, dies in Frankfurt. He is succeeded by his oldest son, John, known as Cicero due to his education and eloquence. As the first sovereign of the March of Brandenburg, John made Berlin-Cölln his place of permanent residence, bringing great prosperity to the city. A police ordinance obliges prostitutes to wear distinctive clothing so that while single young Berlin girls dress in a pretty, virginal crown and married or widowed noblewomen sport their genteel wimple, the ladies of the street must be seen in short coats, no matter what the weather. The punishment for women found guilty of adultery is death, though, for the peace of their soul, prostitutes are to exorcise their "dangerous arrogance" by selling their services to unmarried official craftsmen.

In the early-16th century, trade began to flourish in Berlin-Cölln. Meanwhile, cities in Eastern Germany forming part of the Holy Roman Empire suffered competition from lower-priced foreign products. They were above all concerned by the introduction of English "industry". Berlin's retail and craft trade benefited from the fact that the Elector established his permanent court here and

"Irontooth".

A whistle-stop journey through time

permitted the great traders from southern Germany (such as the houses of Fugger and Welser) to open branches here. Berlin merchants begin to try long-distance trade, but they have to include both profits and losses in their calculations, with the added disadvantage that the main East-West trade route is a long way from the city.

On 15 December 1508, Elector Joachim I Nestor restored many legal powers in Berlin-Cölln, though he reserved for himself the "penal code", covering crimes for most of which the penalty was death. Moreover, the punishments meted out to serious criminals are designed at once to provide the people with entertainment and to serve as a warning: arsonists, thieves, rapists and disturbers of the peace face beheading; the wheel awaits traitors and murderers; women found guilty of witchcraft will be burned alive, whilst forgers will also be burned at the stake. Confessions are obtained in the usual way: with the help of the Iron Maiden (a hollow iron frame shaped like the human body and lined with spikes to impale the victim) or the Spanish Boot (an iron casing with a screw attachment which compressed the calf of the leg, mutilating the tortured prisoner).

Berlin in around 1500: The city with walls and the Marienkirche in the centre (anonymous woodcut, dated around 1880).

In 1510, the persecution of Jews in Berlin and the March of Brandenburg escalates once more: forty unhappy members of the Jewish community are publicly put to death at the city gates. The advantage of the ruling classes' thought, now "humanist", lies principally in the fact that the Jews no longer entertain the bloodthirsty public as before, but are executed "in an orderly way" under the most absurd accusations.

On 6 February 1510, a case of alleged profanation of the sacred host comes before the court. According to the Berlin tribunal, on this day, a Christian potter named Paul Fromm was apprehended in the theft of two gilded hosts from Knoblauch village church in east Havelland, one of which he had allegedly sold to the Jew Salomon for sacrilegious purposes. Under torture, Salomon confesses to cutting the host with a knife, thus dishonouring it, after which more and more Jews are systematically accused of profaning hosts and sacrificing Christian children, and a total of some one hundred people are finally taken to Berlin. Forty who confess under torture are declared guilty by the court: 38 are burned alive whilst the other two, who had converted to Christianity, are granted the mercy of the court and are merely beheaded.

An execution in Berlin: the Rabenstein place of execution, outside the city walls near what is now Straußberger Platz.

On 31 October 1517, the Augustinian monk Martin Luther nails his 95 theses against the practice of selling indulgences to the door of Wittenberg Castle church, whilst the most famed and successful vendor of the day, Johann Tetzel, general sub-commissioner for the sale of these indulgences in the archbishopric of Magdeburg, was raking it in from Berliners in the Church of St Nicholas (Nikolaikirche). Many, their body and soul still "dry" from the last plague, think that it will probably do no good, but neither can it do any harm to try to save themselves a corner in Tetzel's Heaven for a few silver coins, or *Thaler*.

On 2 November 1539, the Reformation reaches Berlin. The change to the doctrines preached by Martin Luther does not occur overnight, however. On 25 February 1537, the preacher John Baderesch is first evangelical parish priest at St Peter's (Petrikirche) in Berlin-Cöllner. Joachim II Hector, Elector of Brandenburg since the death of his father, Joachim I Nestor, had tolerated the gradual conversion of his people to the Lutheran doctrines.

In 1542, Elector Joachim II commissions the architect Caspar Theyß to build a hunting lodge for him in the forest to the west of Berlin, to which he gives the name "Zum grünen Wald" (towards the green wood). It is said that, besides the lodge, which will later become known as Grunewald, the Elector also built a dike over the swampy ground, shoring it up with planks. This path, built from tree trunks, then nameless, is what is now the Kurfürstendamm.

Berlin's first weekly newspaper began to be published in 1617. Handwritten, it has no title, but even so stretches to twelve pages. The favourite stories are gossip relating to witch trials and bankruptcies, but considerable space is also devoted to foreign news.

A whistle-stop journey through time

"Last instance"

In around 1620, a stable hand in the service of Elector George Wilhelm opens a tavern in a house beside the city's medieval walls, near the Nikolai district – the "Wiege Berlins", or "Cradle of Berlin". Until 1900, the tavern bore the wordy name of "Biedermeierstübchen am Glockenspiel" in a reference to the instrument played in the nearby parish church.

(When the impressive palace of justice was built in Littenstraße in the 1890s, the bar was given a new name, and has been known since then as the Zur letzten Instanz – Last orders, or in the last instance – presumably not as a premonition of the death sentences that "Red" Hilde Banjamin would pass down here in the 1950s, but in reference to the legend of how two fighting cocks declared peace here.
At the time of writing in 2006, "Last Instance" is Berlin's oldest restaurant. Its regular customers over the years have included the likes of Heinrich Zille, Alfred Döblin, Hans Fallada, Maxim Gorki, Charlie Chaplin and hundreds of other well-known personalities. Even Napoleon Bonaparte once warmed his feet on the 200-year-old Majolica ceramic stove).

The Thirty Years' War Begins

The Thirty Years War

Swedish soldiers dressed for war, with swords, bows and muskets (period copper engraving).

From 1618 to 1648, all Europe was a battlefield. At first, Berlin remained free from military operations, but the city later fell a victim to imperial war contributions when the Hohenzoller conquered the Swedish kingdom, ruled King Gustavo Adolfo II.

Berlin is forced to pay huge amounts of money. Food becomes short and during the last period in the war the city is brutally sacked and pillaged. The populace refuses to take up arms, as illness and epidemics are widespread. Despair takes hold of the city. Torture and murder become everyday events. All is chaos, but no one comes to the rescue. Little more than half the original population of ten thousand survive.

In their desperation and bitter hour of need, many Berliners overcome their disgust and eat human meat. To this end, they lurk around the gallows that have been set up all over the city. "They cut up hanged bodies and sliced off the meat they hungered for", wrote Adolf Streckfuß, Berlin's leading historian in the 19th century. An agreement was not finally reached for the complete withdrawal of all Swedish troops in Germany until 26 June 1650, after months of negotiation. However, the withdrawal agreed with the Swedes was not carried out because not enough money could be raised to pay the foreign soldiers and their captain. The siege of Berlin and the entire March of Brandenburg therefore continued until 1656.

In 1671, Berlin became international. Elector John George gave refuge to many refugees from the Low Countries in the March of Brandenburg, and some settled in the city. Carpet weavers, pastry bakeries and other highly specialised and skilled shops open. It is estimated that the population of Berlin in 1671 was around 12,000, compared to London and Paris, which each already had more than one hundred thousand inhabitants.

On 21 May 1671, fifty families of Jews expelled from Vienna are allowed to settle in the March of Brandenburg by order of the Great Elector Frederick Wilhelm I. Their dispensation is initially valid for twenty years. Moreover, by paying protection money of eight pounds per year per family, they can also trade freely. And so begins the history of the Jewish community in Berlin. Nonetheless, their protector's edict does not include permission to build a synagogue for religious services, and they must use their houses for this purpose. They can, however, establish a Jewish cemetery, and to this end purchase land at I Große Hamburger Straße (in Mitte).

On 8 November 1685, the Great Elector Frederick Wilhelm I, who died on 9 May 1688, offered refuge in highly favourable conditions to persecuted French Huguenots. They are given freedom of religious faith, citizen's rights and a series of economic privileges. By adopting these measures, the Elector hopes to stimulate economic and cultural development in Brandenburg Prussia.

The edict issued by the Great Elector Frederick Wilhelm to enable Jews expelled from Vienna to live in Germany.

A whistle-stop journey through time

The Great Elector Frederick Wilhelm receives Huguenot refugees (period wood engraving).

Amongst the immigrant Huguenots are many wealthy merchants, businessmen and skilled craftsmen. These newcomers will give fresh impulse to industry in Berlin by introducing new, advanced manufacturing methods, unknown until then in the city. In particular, the immigrants have enormous influence in the textile industry, which prospers to the point where the elegance of mid-17th century French fashions begin to be imitated. In Berlin Mitte (in Dorotheenstraße), a French colony with its own administration, courts, school and advanced public welfare services becomes established. In the early-18th century, Huguenots make up one-fifth of the total population, which grows rapidly in the cities along the Spree (Berlin and surrounding area), its influence apparent above all in a growing taste for elegance.

The latest fashion: ladies in their elegant apparel. Berlin loves France. The influence of the French Revolution and the interest in Greek antiquity will also change the way gentlemen dress.

Women place their orders for the *denier cry* (the latest fashion, or "cry"): tight dresses so low-cut that they leave their breasts practically naked. On their heads, they wear high wimples. Nor are many any longer satisfied with just anything: their new head-wear will be the long curled wig for which King Frederick I, well known for squeezing every possible penny out of his subjects, would invent the "wig tax". Anyone wearing these hairy artworks must obtain a stamp on payment of the corresponding amount. Patrols of tax inspectors went around the city, pulling wigs off heads and confiscating them in the very street if the bearer failed to produce proof of payment of this stamp.

Celebrations for the young royal couple. On 6 May 1701, Frederick I, king of Prussia, Frederick I, brings his young bride to his residence in Berlin-Cölln. A two-hundred cannon salute is fired in their honour as, dressed in purple and gold brocade, they greet the jubilant people.
On 5 April 1705, King Frederick I founds Charlotte burg. This same day, the king gives Lautenberg Castle and the surrounding area the name of Charlotte burg (for the love of his bride, Sophie-Charlotte).
(Three hundred years later, this district will be liberally sprinkled with magnificent buildings from the period of economic boom, historic buildings, museums and theatres, as well as a varied range of restaurants, cafés and nightclubs. This is where we find the city's main thoroughfares: one side of Kurfürstendamm; Kingstree, from Zoo station to the Furniture radio station and the Olympic Stadium; Sandier Dam with the castle and Kaiserdamm; and from Otto-Suhr-Allee avenue to June 17 avenue towards the victory column).
On 25 February 1713, Frederick I, first Prussian king, dies. His son and successor, Frederick Wilhelm I, who will go down in history as the "soldier king", dies on 31 May 1740 at the age of 55. His son, Frederick II, takes over as regent, receiving intact an empire that he will soon turn into a great power.
Frederick II, who likes to play the flute, is a cultured regent of refined taste. Under his rule, an active, hugely tolerant cultural life develops in Berlin. This is where books forbidden in other German principalities are printed. Many scholars and artists move to the city, drawn here by the fame it has won thanks to the king, who also revives the scientific academy, which had been neglected by his predecessors. Frederick is a great admirer of France and its artists and intellectuals, particularly the great French philosopher Voltaire, with whom he spends whole nights locked in conversation at Sanssouci Castle.
At dawn on 28 May 1756, Frederick II leaves Berlin at the head of his army, marching towards Beelitz. This day marks the beginning of the Seven Years' War, which will finally come to an end on 30 March 1763. Thirty thousand Berliners (out of a total population of around one hundred thousand) live on alms.
On 17 August 1786, Frederick II (the Great) dies at Sanssouci at the age of 74 years. He is succeeded on the throne by his nephew of 43, Frederick Wilhelm II, known as "Fat Willie", a lover

Charlottenburg, soon to be Berlin's most prosperous district, was named after Sophie-Charlotte.

A whistle-stop journey through time

of peace and comfort. This king enjoys a surprising and varied love life. When he dies on 16 November 1797, "Fat Willie", leaves his and successor, Frederick Wilhelm III, a state crippled by debt.

On 26 September 1806, King Frederick Wilhelm III demands that France withdraws from the German Rheinland. This impertinent demand is little less than a declaration of war.

On 14 October 1806, the Saxon and Prussian armies are defeated by the French.

In Berlin, no one is prepared to defend the city against the victors. On 27 October 1806, Napoleon I, Emperor of the French, rides under the Brandenburg Gate at the head of the imperial guard and surrounded by smartly uniformed marshals. The Berliners are surprised by the victors' relaxed discipline and cheerful conduct.

On 29 October 1806, Napoleon orders the modernisation and reform of Berlin's administration and constitution. The French occupation ends towards the end of 1808. However, soon after, Prussia is forced to provide the French emperor with a supporting army of 20,000 soldiers for his campaign against Russia, as well as letting French troops pass freely through Berlin. Not only that, but Prussia must also pay for these soldiers to be fed.

"Le Camp Napoleon Bourg": The military encampment set up by the French troops that entered Berlin (drawing, 1808).

Berlin becomes the centre of the March Revolution

Following the French revolution in February, Berlin is shaken in March 1848 by political meetings and violent demonstrations which, enflamed by the reactionary attitude of King Frederick Wilhelm IV and Prussian superiority, leads to a fully-fledged popular uprising with bloody battles on the barricades. The March Revolution leaves 240 dead and more than a thousand injured amongst the civilian population in Berlin, as well as 20 dead and 254 injured amongst the army and police forces.

It had all started in relative calm. The first news of the revolution that had broken out in Paris reached the Prussian capital on February 26. The Berliners' reaction: a series of ultimatums addressed to the king. This political manifesto embraces all the demands in general that the citizens leading the German revolution address to the princes of the different German states. They include: unconditional freedom of the press; complete freedom of expression; an immediate amnesty for all those persecuted and imprisoned for political crimes; unrestricted right of association; equal political rights for all, whatever their religious faith or material wealth; introduction of trial by jury and independence of the judiciary; the people's own freely-elected representatives... all demands that had long burned in the hearts of the Berliners. The king, however, would not even deign to accept the "Address" signed by 6,000 petitioners.

In the afternoon of March 13, violence breaks out between citizens and soldiers between the Brandenburg Gate and the castle after the cavalry charges the peaceful crowd, swords drawn and without prior warning. The first barricades go up and serious confrontations take place over the following days. On March 18, as the uprising gains more and more ground, Frederick Wilhelm IV declares his approval for a wide-ranging series of reforms before ten thousand Berliners assembled in Schlossplatz. As the people acclaim their king and all Berlin begins to celebrate his princely wisdom and understanding, the soldiers open fire on the crowd. Panic breaks out. Fury against this "betrayal of the people" spreads like wildfire all over the city. On March 19, after the fighting has gone on for 14 hours, the king orders his troops to withdraw.

On 2 January 1861, Frederick Wilhelm IV dies in a state of dementia. His brother, Prussian crown prince Wilhelm, at the age of 60 years, is proclaimed the regent on 9 October 1858.

King Wilhelm I of Prussia is proclaimed as the German emperor on 18 January 1871, and Otto von Bismarck is named Chancellor of the new empire, whose capital is Berlin. That same year, Berlin is affected by an unhealthy economic "boom": rapidly increasing economic growth is suddenly reversed in October 1873 by a sharp, sudden fall in exchange rates.

Life for Jews became harder under Frederick II. In 1768, Frederick increased the "protection tax" that all Jews had to pay every year from fifteen to twenty-five thousand pounds. This measure was aimed not only at bolstering the state coffers, but also at making Berlin less attractive to Jews. The Jewish Community was now answerable for all its members' actions, whether it was a robbery or a blameless bankruptcy.

The Berlin writer Fritz Phillip describes all this in his memoirs: "Everything was created at breakneck speed: building societies and banks in grand buildings, railways and upholsterers, textile and leather factories, petrol and plywood, brick factories and shipyards, companies, association, construction firms and property developers. Everything that was not already nailed down was created. And everyone, absolutely everyone flew towards the light and danced in this frantic race to adore the gilded calf: the wily capitalist and the naïve petit bourgeois, the general and the waiter, the woman of the world, the poor piano teacher and the woman with a stall at the market. Speculation went on in doorways and theatre lobbies, in artists' studios and in the apprentice's quiet home, the coachman and 'Aujuste' in the kitchen followed the ups and downs of events with... feverish interest... Golden rain fell on the inebriated city ... Berlin was living it up in style. Berlin gave itself up to enjoyment and drained the cup of life."

He loved pomp, opulence and ostentation: Emperor Wilhelm II.

Then, suddenly, everything lost its shine. Twenty-eight banks went bankrupt. In his study of the period, Friedrich Engels writes: "Unfortunately, the day of the crack showed that there were not enough consumers for this enormous production."

On 11 May 1878, Emperor Wilhelm I escapes unharmed from an assassination attempt. It occurs during his daily drive in his open carriage. As he approaches the Russian Embassy in Unter den Linden three shots are fired, all missing their target. The gunman is quickly arrested. It turns out to be an unemployed carpenter with extreme political views. The press publishes the rumour that a social democrat plot lies behind the attack. The would-be assassin is tried by an extraordinary court and executed soon afterwards in Moabit. Just three weeks later, on June 2, shots are fired at the 81-year-old monarch once more, and this time Wilhelm is seriously wounded in the head and arms by 30 gun pellets. This time, the assassination attempt is carried out by an unemployed academic who commits suicide after the shooting.

On 9 March 1888, Wilhelm I dies at the age of 91 in his Berlin Palace in Unter den Linden. The cause of death is a slight catarrh. His son, Frederick, 57 years old, succeeds Wilhelm on the throne, but he is already dying from throat cancer. Frederick III reigns for just 99 days. His son will be the last German emperor: Wilhelm II.

Long before the tragic death of his father, a man of liberal ideas, it was no secret that Wilhelm II would govern Germany differently. In fact, whilst Emperor Wilhelm I was well-known for his quiet lifestyle, his grandson Wilhelm delighted in luxury of all kind, sparing no expense in commissioning his preening self-portrait.

In December 1898, Berlin had been hit by food shortages and misery. The economic crisis sparked off by constant excess production since around 1890 has a devastating effect in the capital. In 1893, 400,000 men are sleeping in shelters for the homeless. The unemployed demonstrate or beg. Workers still being paid and able to buy bread must tighten their belts as their wages are cut time and again. Men earn between 9 and 24 marks a week, whilst women receive half this hunger wage. The social democrats, at a meeting in Berlin, call in vain for more jobs to be created, for the construction of public buildings and the hiring of more people to clean the city streets.

...to die of cold and hunger.

On 22 March 1891, Emperor Wilhelm II, in the presence of his entire family, lays the first stone in the church at the end of Kurfürstendamm that will bear his name (the church is consecrated two years later. With its 113-metre-high tower, it will remain the highest building in the city for many years).

At the turn of the century (1899-1900), Kurfürstendamm has the aspect of a showcase for Imperial tastes. The boulevard, with all its pomp and glory, is converted more into a street of houses, with fewer shops. Aristocratic mansions, practically palaces, most with five floors, richly adorned with doorways over three metres high and lobbies faced in marble, wide staircases and artistically decorated lifts. King-sized luxury homes (300-400 m^2)

with 10 or 15 bedrooms or more, with costly ceilings. And at
the rear, amid gardened interior courtyards, are the shamefully
narrow service doors 10.

Great mansions for Berlin's
rich burghers.

What is Hollywood?

Something never before seen, anywhere in the world! On 1 November 1895, the eccentric Max Skladanowsky places on show
for the first time his "living photographs" at Berlin's Wintergarten,
the variety theatre on Friedrichstrasse with Dorotheenstraße.
Thus it is that this "winter garden" becomes the first cinema in
Germany. Skladanowsky had invested three years' ingenuity and
sophisticated development in inventing and developing his recording and projection equipment. Using this double projector – known
as the bioscope – it is possible to alternatively print two films and
show them on the screen. Before an enthusiastic audience of
1,500 spectators, the inventor shows his 3- and 4-metre long
films on an endless loop. The short scenes feature dances, fights
and juggling acts. Already, in 1892, Skladanowsky had begun to
create still shots of his brother Emil doing physical exercise. His
camera is equipped with a mechanism that freezes movements
into numerous single photographs.
He applies for a loan in order to build a projector that will enable
him to show his films to larger audiences, but his application is
turned down. In his state of need, this misunderstood genius is
reduced to cutting individual shots from his films and flicking
them with his thumb. This so called "pocket cinema", films shown
on the fingers, is an enormous success, and the proceeds from
it enable him to fund his new projector.

On 3 March 1904, with a population of around one million, Berlin is the city in the world with the most houses for rent. Most immigrant workers and even many born and bred here are forced to live in slums, rotten housing shared by too many inhabitants with up to six interior courtyards and millions of rats but neither light nor air.

"...the height of social decadence." Berlin Cathedral was consecrated in 1905.

In the view of Emperor Wilhelm II, Berlin's new cathedral, consecrated on 27 December 1905, is the "cathedral of German Protestantism". However, for its critics, who quickly emerge, the construction symbolises the "high watermark of decadence". The new cathedral is named after a church demolished here, in Schlossplatz, in 1747. The first cathedral was built between 1745 and 1750 and reconstructed in neo-classical style by Karl Friedrich von Schinkel in 1817 and 1820-21. In 1893, this building was demolished to be replaced by a new cathedral more to the taste of Emperor Wilhelm II.

A whistle-stop journey through time

All Berlin laughs because of an unemployed shoemaker. On 16 October 1906, Wilhelm Voigt, miserably poor, his reputation in tatters due to certain spells in prison and embittered by the arrogance and capricious nature of the imperial authorities, dresses his thin body in a uniform bought second hand for a bargain price. He takes command as "captain" over ten soldiers from the First Guards regiment he encounters marching alongside him by coincidence and orders them to accompany him by train to Köpenick. Once there, still commanding his troops, he enters the town hall and, after arresting the mayor, makes for the passport office because, in order to turn him back on a homeland that does not want him, he needs the passport he has until now been denied due to the most spurious reasons. However, there is no such office at Köpenick town hall. When he finds out, the false captain empties the municipal coffers.

The case, which will later inspire Carl Zuckmayer to write his play *The Captain from Köpenick*, makes headline news, with all and sundry laughing fit to burst at the Prussian people's obsession with uniform and blind obedience to the authorities. Prussia – as everyone knows – is not a geographic region, but a philosophy of life, an ineffable image of the human being and the world that now falls into ridicule and, above all, reveals the spiritual weakness of its arrogant propagandists.

In spring 1907, when KaDeWe (department store of the West) opens in Tauentzien, Berlin boasts a veritable palace selling the largest, most expensive and luxurious items. Almost at the same time, the equally famous luxury Hotel Adlon opens in Pariser Platz.

Captain Köpenick gets into a carriage on his release from prison in 1909.

Albert Einstein reaches Zoo Station

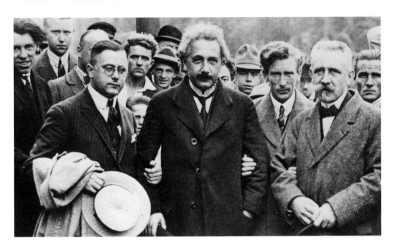

Albert Einstein at a peaceful demonstration against the war in Berlin on 29 July 1923.

On 29 March 1914, he gets off the train from Aquisgrán, little knowing that he will spend the next 19 years in Berlin. He is as yet unaware, too, that he will soon become internationally known because here, in Berlin, is where he will establish his General Theory of Relativity. Young Albert Einstein, 35 years of age, arrives to take up his place at the Prussian Science Academy. In return, he will receive 12,000 a year. But it is not the money that has drawn him to Berlin. Years earlier, he had fallen in love with his cousin, Elsa Löwenthal. Einstein would later write to her that: "What was most wonderful were our walks in Grunewald and, when the weather was bad, the time we spent in your room."

Emperor Wilhelm II surrounded by his soldiers.

Berlin mobilised. The German Empire enthusiastically heads towards the First World War

On 31 July 1914, in Unter den Linden, before the statue of Frederick the Great, an army officer announces to the assembled crowd that there is a "state of danger of imminent war." The next day at 5 pm, at the city castle gate, by order of the Emperor, a guard announces general mobilisation. The newspapers report that "the multitude, deeply moved, sang as one whilst the bells rang out *Nun danket alle Gott* (Give thanks to God)". These days, Berliners in their thousands go about the city enthralled by authentic warlike delirium. Speeches are given everywhere and the cry of "Long Live the Emperor" is heard all over the city. Thousands of men enlist as volunteers to go to the front. Warning voices are silenced amid the general excitement. A few groups of social democrats attempt to organise strikes and protest demonstrations. Unsuccessfully. "Deutschland, Deutschland über alles

Germany!" (Germany over all!) is the cry that rings out from most throats.

The year 1917 is marked by growing political unrest and general strikes against food shortages, the war and the Emperor. Food rations are smaller every day, prices ever higher, energy supplies scarce and the fact that no ending to a war that has brought with it a terrible death toll seems to be in sight further fuels discontent amongst the population. In February, even the weapons factories are hit by strikes. "Dogs, those that go on strike whilst our armies are facing the enemy" shouts the head of war organisation in his rage. Then, Berlin suffers the worst winter in many years. The daily ration for adults is 270 g bread, ? of one egg, 11 g butter and 35 g meat (including bone). And that is only in theory, as the reality is that not even this much can be found in the shops.

Those volunteering for the army thought the war would be a calk-walk ...

One of the many railway carriages sent off to the front.

Long live the revolution!

When, on 28 January 1918, the people take to the streets in their need, radical forces hope that here too, in Germany, a revolutionary movement similar to that which brought about the October Revolution in Russia, will take shape. Emperor Wilhelm II meets force with force: on February 1, Berlin is declared under a state of emergency. The army attempts to restore order. All meetings are banned. Anyone who fails to return to work by February 4 is threatened with immediate transfer to the front line of death.

At noon on 9 November 1918 – the decisive moment and high point of the November Revolution – the Imperial Chancellor, Prince Max von Baden, announces the abdication of Emperor Wilhelm II and his succession on the throne by Crown Prince Frederick Wilhelm.

Nr. 263
Berliner Zeitung
42. Jahrgang

1 Uhr
Sonnabend,
9. November 1918.

Der Kaifer hat abgedankt.

Thronverzicht des Kronprinzen — Ebert wird Reichskanzler — Einberufung einer Nationalversammlung

The press published the
unbelievable...
"The Chancellor has abdicated"

Forced by the incendiary situation in the capital, von Baden is anticipating the emperor's final decision in this statement, as it is still possible that Wilhelm may opt not to abdicate. No one mourns the inglorious ending to the German monarchy. At noon, the Imperial Chancellor appoints as his successor the SPD president Friedrich Ebert. Workers' and soldiers' councils are formed at factories and in the barracks.

At around 2 pm, Philipp Scheidemann, president of the SPD parliamentary group, proclaims the German Republic from a window of the Parliament building. Soon after this, Karl Liebknecht proclaims the Free Socialist Republic from a balcony in Berlin Castle. This double proclamation of republics eloquently illustrates the contradiction between the November Revolution and the different interests of the parties involved. The social democrats appear to have achieved their goals: the fall of the former authoritarian state, the establishment of a parliamentary democracy and the union between workers and the bourgeoisie. The left, led by Liebknecht and Rosa Luxemburg, wants a Soviet-style socialist republic. On November 10, Friedrich Ebert forms a provisional government with the approval of the workers' and soldiers' councils.

The First World War ends

On 10 November 1918, the imperial court leaves the country, making for the Dutch border. Emperor Wilhelm II is given asylum in the Low Countries. Meanwhile, in Berlin, Friedrich Ebert has taken up his post as imperial chancellor.

In this way, one of the conditions agreed under the armistice negotiations is fulfilled: the replacement of the monarchy by a government elected by the people. On November 11, the delegate for the Weimar Republic in Compiègne Wood signs the conditions laid out by the French Marshal Ferdinand Foch.

The Weimar Republic

At an empire-wide conference which takes place in the Prussian chamber of representatives on 1 January 1919, the 127 delegates from the Spartacist League, the Red Soldiers League, the Young Free Socialists and the International Communists agree to dissolve the Independent Social Democrat Party (USDP in German) and to found the German Communist Party (KPD in German). The leaders of the new KPD are Rosa Luxemburg, Karl Liebknecht and Wilhelm Pieck. On January 5, the Spartacists occupy the Kochstraße publishing district and call for insurrection. The government, presided over by Friedrich Ebert, responds by imposing a state of emergency. Troops are ordered to storm the district. The uprising comes to a bloody end over the days and nights of January 11 and 12.

Rosa Luxemburg, born in Poland, 48 years of age, and Karl Liebknecht, 47, former member of parliament (co-founders of the KPD), are arrested on the afternoon of 15 January 1919 at the Hotel Eden on the Kurfürstendamm, brutally treated by the soldiers and shot in the back on the way to Moabit remand prison. The killers throw Rosa Luxemburg's body into the canal.

On 19 January 1919, elections to the national constituent assembly take place. The SPD continues to be the strongest party by a large margin. Right-wing parties obtain just 63 out of 421 seats. The national assembly is convened in Weimar on February 6. The transfer of such an important institution to the provincial capital causes a massive protest amongst Berlin municipal councillors. In his speech to the opening of the parliament in Weimar, Friedrich Ebert explains the move by allusion to the

Rosa Luxemburg with Karl Liebknecht on their way to the demonstration that took place days before their murder.

great, classical Weimar tradition of Goethe and Schiller, to the Germany of poets and philosophers, as opposed to the antiquated traditions of Prussian, military Berlin. But this is nothing more than a pretext. The real motive is much less idealist: Berlin continues to be insecure ground, and the threat of disturbances still hangs in the air (thus, as simply and, at heart, illogically as this is how the idea for the Weimar Republic came into being).

The Versailles Peace Treaty

A gloomy sextet: the German delegation to Versailles.

From left to right: Schücking, Giesberts, Landsberg, Brockdorff-Rantzau, Leinert and Melchior.

The Versailles Peace Treaty: for many Germans, the beginning of the Second World War. At 3.12 pm, five years after the Austrian Archduke Franz Ferdinand was assassinated in a shooting that signalled the start of the Great War, the German delegation signs a peace treaty dictated by the victorious powers. These have rejected practically all German requests and have confirmed their demand for the German emperor and all leaders of the former imperial government to be handed over to them. The German Chancellor, Philipp Scheidemann, who resigns rather than accept the terms of the Treaty of Versailles, attacks it as "a temporary sentence of death for Germany", going on to declare that "Only a treaty that can be fulfilled, that keeps us alive... can rebuild Germany... Down with the murder plan", he exclaims in his indignation.

Germany is forced to surrender 70,000 square kilometres and 7.3 million citizens. Moreover, it must hand over a large part of its annual production: 75% of zinc and iron mined and 28% of coal, as well as 20% of its already low potato and cereal harvests. Germany is also banned from imposing compulsory military service and the strength of the country's army and navy is greatly reduced. The country is also to pay huge reparations, whose exact amount is not established in the treaty.

A whistle-stop journey through time

The assassination of Walter Rathenau

It is the 376th political assassination in Germany since 1919: on 24 June 1922, Foreign Minister Walter Rathenau is the victim of a cowardly killing.

The incident occurs during Rathenau's journey from his villa in Königsallee to the Foreign Ministry. A gunman in a vehicle following the minister's open-top car opens fire with a machine-gun. A second assassin throws a hand grenade into the car. Rathenau, who jumps up when the killers turn their weapons on him, dies immediately. Walter Rathenau, son of Emil, the founder of AEG (Allgemeine Elektrizitätsgesellschaft) electrical-engineering company was in charge of the German war economy under Emperor Wilhelm II. Before his assassination, the victorious powers had slandered him as a "ruthless executor" and a "hired gun", though it seems that it was actually Rathenau who argued most forcefully for a reduction in the reparations that Germany was forced to pay. One of the ultra-right wing tirades against Germany's first and only Jewish foreign minister ended with a verse translating as "Shoot Walter Rathenau, the damned Jewish pig."

(The assassins, identified a few days after the shooting, are members of the CONSUL terrorist organisation. One is shot by the police, whilst the other commits suicide).

Walter Rathenau

Prosperous Berlin becomes a cosmopolitan city

After 500 years of Hohenzoller rule, Berlin is free, and not only of the constraints imposed by the monarchy. The city breathes in deeply, generating unsuspected energy. In the 1920s, Berlin was the leading industrial city on the entire continent. It was also the main centre for trade and banking, as well as boasting the most important stock exchange. Europe's principal railway hub, it is also the German Empire's second-most important inland port. Nearly half the employed population (48%) work in industry, whilst 30.5% are civil servants and private sector workers.

In the working-class districts – Wedding, Moabit, Prenzlauer Berg and Neukölln – we are beginning to see the structures for a new "form of society", unknown here as yet, but long-established in the United States: organised crime. Bands of thieves, fences and black marketeers begin to form, camouflaged as "savings societies". The Berlin crime squads rearm, becoming what is considered for many years to be the finest criminal police force in the world.

With the opening of Tempelhof Airport (1924), Berlin is "Europe's aerial crossroads" with its vast trade and exhibition sites and the radio tower erected in 1926 joins the tiny club of truly cosmopolitan cities around which just about everything generally revolves. Berlin's "supremacy" is based on teaching everyone everything possible, endlessly, playing the lead role and establishing itself as a model to be followed in politics, economics, art and culture.

Little Max Klante: a giant amongst confidence tricksters

Soon after the end of the Great War, this brush manufacturer buys a camera and makes himself known as an "artistic photographer", though he is completely unsuccessful in this. Then he sets up a betting shop, and suddenly his luck turns and he begins to make money, after which he becomes unstoppable. Max Klante weaves his web amongst those of slender means, who see him as a gift from heaven. He establishes Max Klante & Co. GmbH, a company whose official mission is to set up a racing stable and stud farm in order to promote horse-breeding in Germany. He pretends to have great contacts amongst the leading betting shops in the German Empire, claiming to have invented a practically infallible system by which it is possible to make enormous profits from horse racing.

Max Klante, one-time brush manufacturer, became the biggest swindler Berlin has ever known.

From his own magazine, *Meldereiter*, Klante tells his readers: "You give me whatever seems reasonable as a monthly loan, which you can cease to pay whenever you want. The depositor runs no risk of making a loss, and will receive 600% interest every month. So, at the end of the month, you receive seven times the original amount loaned."
Many trust him and put all their savings into his hands. The seductive Klante can win people over like nobody's business: "I appeal to all those who have been hurt by fate to exercise their rights", he proclaims, "I want to bring together all those whom the government has forgotten. They must have the same opportunities as the masters of great capital fortunes ..."

It is just that the same opportunities as the loan sharks who lurk in international waters have been accorded to one determined to rise to the top, as fast as possible: Max Klante buys a modern office block, opens branch offices in other large cities and establishes a special window for police officers at Dresden police station, where long queues form. The people, who call him "Comrade", look on him as their saviour, praising him to high heaven: "All Berlin sings out in unison. On, on, let us go with Klante!" Crowds cheer him wherever he goes.
(In early-1921, whilst Adolf Hitler has won over no more than around 900 followers, 260,000 Berliners had entrusted Max

Klante with their savings). For months, everything goes perfectly, because Klante is lucky at the races and can pay the interest on the new amounts of money he constantly receives. By now, he owns half a dozen fine mansions, whilst the Klante jockey team, with their blue jackets with yellow stripes, advertise his services. Klante has also amassed three luxurious limousines, has his own valet and spoils more than a dozen lovers.

But suddenly, overnight, his empire collapses. Klante is arrested on the morning of 21 September 1921, despite his attempts to escape detention by checking into a health clinic. At this moment, his rapidly accumulating debt stands at around 92 million gold marks.

Klante's "betting bank" in Berlin in 1921.

The trial begins on 11 December 1922. Max Klante is carried into court on a stretcher. A young woman throws herself weeping over him, and has to be dragged away by force. Other women clasp handkerchiefs. The victims of his fraudulent activities boo and jeer whilst his lawyers state the case for the defence. Then the sentence is passed down: three years in prison. Few can contain their rage and indignation.

But Klante can survive practically anything, even the Second World War. The only thing he cannot take is his descent into poverty. On the door to his squalid flat in a half-ruined building near the Alexanderplatz in 1945 is a cardboard sign reading: "Max Klante, brush maker". In 1955, his flatmates find him dead. He has taken his own life.

An illustrative example from the 1920s. Berlin is infested with impostors, forgers, con-men... This was a period when crooks and criminals were able to amass huge wealth and riches.

Gennart of the murder squad, on the trail of all criminals

This is the date chosen by Adolf Köster, *Reich* interior minister, to present an imperial criminal law that will lead, in years to come, to a revolution in the way crime is fought.

Considerable merit must be placed in this at the feet of Ernst Gennart, director of the Berlin murder squad. Gennart, who weighed 150 kilos, is considered the father of scientific criminology. The authorities especially converted an enormous six-seater Daimler-Benz for Gennart and his murder squad, the features in this legendary vehicle including an office and a chemical laboratory. Wherever this great monster, black as a crow, parked, something terrible had happened. The car greatly impressed citizens. Gennart, a confirmed bachelor, had only two passions: to consume enormous amounts of coffee and cakes, and his legendary criminal investigation file, which he himself had "invented". He collected information not only on all cases falling under his authority in Berlin, but also full documentation on capital crimes throughout the Reich and internationally. His reasoning was a simple as it was acute: the police can only fight crime effectively if they know how criminals act down to the last detail. From this information, we can establish patterns amongst the authors of crimes and their actions.

Gennart's mysterious file is a favourite topic amongst criminalists all over the world, and he is duly obliged to receive visitors from practically all countries to show them his work. From 1918 to 1939, when he died, Ernst Gennart solved a total of 298 murders, including many that appeared impossible to unravel.

(when, in 1945, the Americans found part of Gennart's collection of criminal records, unique in the world at that time, they were awestruck, and an FBI expert was forced to confess that he had never before seen anything so perfect in the field).

Commissioner Gennart

"Organised crime" in Berlin poses in apparent harmless harmony in the 1920s.

The members of the "Sport- und Geselligkeitsverein Immertreu 1919 e.V." club, seen here on their annual day out, were not blameless citizens, for this was an association of former convicts that held criminal sway over Berlin's social life for many years.

A whistle-stop journey through time

The "roaring 20s"...

Throughout the so-called "roaring 20s", Berlin was in its heyday as a centre of intellectual and cultural life: more than 35 theatres, several opera houses and over 20 concert halls attracted tens of thousands of spectators every day.

Berlin: the city attracted and gave shelter to writers and artists from all over the empire, as well as many foreigners.

These five personalities can well be taken to represent hundreds more like them (from left to right): the Saxon Heinrich Zille, the most "Berlin" draughtsman the city will ever had; Carl Zuckmayer, playwright from Rheinhessen, Carl Zuckmayer; the Saxon author Erich Kästner; Alfred Kerr, a critic from Silesia; and the Berlin painter Max Lieberman.

Berlin is where internationally famed artists live, including such avant-garde painters as Otto Nagel, Karl Hofer, Max Pechstein, George Grosz, Otto Dix and writers of the calibre of Bertolt Brecht, Alfred Döblin, Heinrich Mann, Gottfried Benn and Kurt Tucholsky. Many successful publishers and journalists, artists and directors also make their home in the capital. Even Germany's largest film production company, UFA, has its headquarters in Berlin (many German film stars, directors and cameramen emigrated after 1933, seeking to start a new life and career in Hollywood).

Berlin is the leading city even when it comes to the press, and more than 150 dailies and weeklies are published in the capital. There are two editions per day for the Berlin paper BZ, considered the quickest tabloid in the world to hit the streets.

By 1 October 1920, the population of Greater Berlin has reached nearly four million distributed over an area of around 900 square kilometres (larger than Paris or London). This area is divided into 320 districts of differing size, and the exterior districts, previously independent, have now been absorbed into the city.

On 29 October 1923, the Berliner Rundfunk radio station begins its broadcasts (Attention, attention! You are listening to Voxhaus Berlin on the 400 waveband!"). There are fine hotels, luxury department stores, cafeterias, restaurants, bars, variety halls and elegant nightclubs all over the city, and Berlin's nightlife is legendary. Meanwhile, pubs and brothels abound in the working-class districts, and cheap variety theatres enable many, even the less well-off, to forget the miseries of their lives, at least for a few hours.

Inflation: Berlin nightmare

But in the shade of the brilliantly-illuminated magnificent city boulevards and plazas lurks the threat of misery and ruin. Striking suddenly, it engulfs all and sundry in its perilous floodwaters. Inflation has broken out!
Since April 1923, the situation in Berlin has worsened considerably, and the city is now benighted by mass misery and social conflict. A decree eloquently illustrates the grotesque situation that exists in the city: gourmet restaurants and dancehalls are requisitioned to establish soup kitchens and to provide the homeless with shelter from the cold. But foreign currencies can still buy just about anything: German and foreign speculators alike live in the lap of luxury. The "humble" people seek distraction in cheaper pleasures, and sales of alcohol and other drugs sky-rocket.

Travelling salesmen: opportunistic Berliners selling a "Schnapps substitute" on the streets.

Those not amongst Berlin's 250,000 unemployed are forced to watch their pay shrink day by day. In October 1923, it takes a skilled worker nine hours labour to earn enough to buy a pound of margarine. Every morning, the banknotes printed at the Ullstein works in Kochstraße are paid out in suitcase-loads. Those receiving this money then run as quickly as they can to the nearest shop in order to buy food or other small items before the money loses its value. On 15 November 1923, the *rentenmark* is issued to replace the practically worthless paper money, marking the beginning of the end of the inflationist nightmare. On November 20, the exchange rate is set at 1 US dollar = 4.2 billion *papiermark*. One *rentenmark* is worth a million *papiermark*. The worst is over.

A whistle-stop journey through time

In the Jewish East

On 7 July 1924, a hot summer's day, Joseph Roth, a journalist and writer who arrived in Berlin from Galicia in 1920 and in time became one of the best-paid journalists in the Weimar Republic, visits the Jewish quarter in Scheunenviertel, as many curious people do every day.

The air of the narrow streets here is thick with the most varied aromas. The area smells of fried onion and boiled fish, of hot fat, of unknown spices, of ripe apples and recently-washed nappies. Though, if the wind is in the wrong direction, it is better to hold one's nose: a truly terrible stink wafts over from the nearby open drainage channels. However, today, the wind is favourable. All the doors and windows are wide open. The sound of someone playing the violin carries down into the street. There are signs written in Hebrew on doors and in shop windows. Herring sells, along with gramophone records, second-hand books and a vast miscellany of knick-knacks.

Jewish quarter: a street scene in the 1920s.

The Ghetto, full of life yet oddly sad, is inhabited emigrant Jews from Eastern Europe. Many have fled from the pogroms in Russia or from persecution in Poland. In their long black coats and black hats, under which we can see wisps of snow-white hair and long flowing beards, the Jews come and go along Grenadierstraße, usually in the road rather than along the pavement. There, in the dark shadows of a house entrance, is someone murmuring, whispering. Saying their prayers quickly, hands trembling, the prayer seems endless. No one bothers them.

A whistle-stop journey through time

Everywhere are small businesses that can be conducted without the need for a shop. Huge, thoughtful eyes, majestic old heads, timeless, wise. Chess is just played as an excuse; what is important is to chat. Women and children meet around the fruit and vegetable stalls. Public life here makes one forget that one is in the middle of Berlin, the busiest city in the world. Here, there seems to be a deep, practically bottomless hole in the dizzy, noisy, bustling metropolis, a well into which the imaginative visitor can gaze, amazed, at the eternal human essence. And even so, only one-third of the Jewish community lives in Grenadierstraße, considered the main street for Eastern Jews. And the percentage is falling constantly. Many emigrants have been expelled, some have managed to escape to America, whilst others have become Berliners. What will remain is the myth.

By the early-1920s, the original Scheunenviertel (granary district) no longer existed. Its name alludes to the granaries built here after an ordinance was passed in 1672 to the effect that all inflammable materials should be stored outside Berlin, there on the site where the popular theatre now stands. It was the victim of imperial town planning.

1923: books on sale at the entrance to the "EZ-Chajim" Talmud-Tora school at 31, Grenadierstraße.

Let's go, let's go! There's no time, there's no time!

The "roaring 20s" is the most dizzyingly fast period in Germany's history. Newspapers, films, love affairs, even murders… everything takes place in record time. Nowhere else do so many things happen, nowhere else does the never-before-seen take place in such quick sequence. Bustling, busy Berlin takes over everyone, people say that being in Berlin is like drinking champagne. Even those who, inexplicably, fail to enter into the general madness will nevertheless inescapably be infected in the end, becoming addicted and forming part of the myth called Berlin. Despite all this, however, Berlin has many and varied faces.

On 5 November 1923, a group of people attack Scheunenviertel, in the old town of Berlin, beating up many inhabitants, East European Jews, and ransacking Jewish shops. The disturbances caused by these anti-Semitic agitators are the consequence of general unrest and insecurity caused by the monetary crisis. Many angry, frustrated people are willing to believe the rumour that Eastern Jewish speculators are becoming rich thanks to inflation. Police cordon off the district, but the attacks last the whole night, continuing into the next day.

The Jewish writer Franz Kafka chose Berlin as his last place of residence.

A whistle-stop journey through time

In the heart of the Scheunenviertel: View of Grenadierstraße from Münzstraße.

Cover of Hitler's book "My Struggle".

On 26 November 1923, Franz Kafka moves to Berlin, a city that has fascinated him since he visited it with his then fiancée Felice Bauer in 1913. The writer establishes his home with his new fiancée, Dora Diamant, at 8, Steglitzer Miquelstraße.

Hitler's mask slips

The first edition of *Mein Kampf* ("My Struggle"), the book he wrote whilst in prison in Landsberger (July 1924), is published on 18 July 1925. The 400-page volume costs 12 marks. In it, Hitler presents what is, more or less, his manifesto. Proclaiming his right to take power he makes no bones about his political objectives. Nor does he attempt to hide his fanatical anti-Semitism: he openly declares his goal of establishing a totalitarian national-socialist state united by race, as well as vindicating Germany's right to unlimited expansion into Eastern Europe (9,473 copies of the book are sold before the year's end).

A whistle-stop journey through time

The Nazis

On 1 November 1926, Joseph Goebbels takes over leadership of
the National Socialist German Workers' Party (the Nazi Party, or
NSDAP, in German) in the Berlin-Brandenburg district. The Berlin
branch was established on 17 February 1925, whilst Berlin SA
and SS (militias founded by Hitler, the former later eclipsed by the
latter) associations are founded in 1926.

Goebbels begins the "struggle for the Empire's red capital",
attempting to enlist the Berlin working classes to this end. On
November 14, leads the first great SA propaganda march
through "red" Neukölln to Halleschen Tor. Many of the 320 SA
men are injured in the street fights that break out, as the Nazi
movement creates its own martyrs.

Hitler's terrible propaganda
genius: Joseph Goebbels.

Hitler in Berlin

On 1 May 1927, Adolf Hitler gives his first speech to the Berlin
branch of the NSDAP at the Clou concert hall at 25, Kreuzberger Mauerstraße. As the NSDAP leader is banned from giv-
ing public addresses in Prussia, he speaks to a meeting of party
members behind closed doors. Though the meeting at the Clou
concert hall goes off without incident, a few days later violence
breaks out at a NSDAP public meeting. At the "solder's social
centre" in Chausseestraße, a parish priest constantly heckles
Goebbels during his speech, and is ejected brutally. This act of
violence is followed by more and more serious incidents between
anti-Nazi protesters and the police, with many left dead and
injured on either side.

A whistle-stop journey through time

...hope and hunger in the city streets.

On 1 May 1929, violent confrontation takes place between Communist workers and police in Mitte, Neukölln and Wedding. The result is 32 dead, more than 300 injured and 1,200 arrested. This is followed by the darkest chapter in the history of the capital of the Weimar Republic.

25 October 1929: the Wall Street stock exchange crash unleashes a terrible economic crisis whose repercussions are felt in Berlin in the shape of unemployment higher than ever before known. By the beginning of the following year the jobless total 300,000 (in spring 1932, employment will stand at 600,000 in Berlin). The immediate consequences are mass demonstrations. The ground could not have been better prepared for the Nazis. Very few people amongst those who have fallen once more into a state of misery and poverty have salvaged the vain hope that things will get better again.

Berlin continues to resist the Nazi terror

The countless problems and crises that Germany had faced since the First World War now throw a huge shadow over events that would follow: even before Hitler rose to power, the University of Berlin had long been affected by extreme right-wing violence. All most students appeared indifferent to politics, throwing themselves fully into their studies or earning themselves a living, those that were active were largely right-wingers and extreme right-wingers. Even towards the end of the 1920s, the Nazis were winning great support amongst students, who practised daily, systematic terror against their Jewish classmates.

Fear is eating into the very souls of many Berliners. And even so, even after the Hitlerian creed had spread like the plague all over Germany, the people of Berlin continued to mount serious opposition against the Nazis. The peculiar characteristics attributed to Berliners in Imperial times, their quick powers of understanding and their much-feared tongue made it difficult for Hitler's propaganda to work on them. Those closest to the *Führer* would often let it be known, quietly, that Hitler had great respect for Berlin. The facts show that, despite their awesome propaganda machine, the Nazis only made headway very slowly n the city. The even lost votes here between July and November 1932, their 25.9% quota clearly lower than the average for the rest of the empire which stood at 33%. Even when, on 30 January 1933, Goebbels organised celebrations for Hitler's appointment as imperial chancellor in the shape of a torch-lit parade lasting hours, superbly stage managed around the

Brandenburg Gate, this did not at first change much with regard to the Berliners' mixture of scepticism and outright rejection.

Berlin celebrates power takeover

On 30 January 1933, more than 15,000 National Socialists and their followers celebrate Adolf Hitler's appointment as imperial chancellor. Victory celebrations take place all over Berlin. The National Socialists know it: they have won, the state is theirs. In the evening, the "national groups" – SA, SS and Steel Helmets – march in a great torch-lit procession along the Charlottenburger Chaussee, passing through the Brandenburg Gate to the Chancellery building in Wilhelmstraße.

On 30 January 1933, the German president, Paul von Hindenburg, is forced to appoint NSDAP leader Adolf Hitler as imperial chancellor. Just a few weeks before, the unwitting Hindenburg had boasted amongst his inner circle "In three months I will have smashed Hitler". The eight national conserva-tive ministers, mostly experts in their respective fields, are joined by just three National Socialists: Hitler, the former postcard artist, recently freed from prison; Wilhelm Frick, interior minis-ter; and Hermann Göring, minister without portfolio. Nonetheless, Göring also doubles as the Prussian interior minis-ter with regard to all police activities within the huge country that is Germany. For this reason, Hindenburg is certain that the NSDAP representatives will soon find themselves "surrounded" and outnumbered by the non-nationalists and that it will be possi-ble to repel their attempt to seize power.

The "stocks":
Public exhibition of an "Arian" woman who has got mixed up with Jews, "race shame" and Jews who sleep with non-Jewish women.

Celebrations for Hitler's rise to power in 1936: SA salute at the Brandenburg Gate.

With Adolf Hitler installed as imperial chancellor, the NSDAP and their followers begin a campaign of terror against their political opponents in Berlin. Communists and social democrats continue to hold the balance of power in several districts in the capital. Every day, Nazi assault troops cause fights in the chambers and in the streets, causing many injuries and even more than one death. On 10 May 1933, the National Socialists and their student followers burn some 20,000 books in the Opernplatz.

This book-burning is the culminating point in an "action against the non-German spirit" launched by propaganda minister Joseph Goebbels. The aim of this campaign is to bring public opinion into line, persecuting any intellectual who dares to think differently, and to impregnate the universities with National Socialist doctrines. From now on, many works by outstanding writers will be considered "non-German" and therefore banned. These include such authors as the brothers Heinrich and Thomas Mann, Arthur Schnitzler, Kurt Tucholsky, Arnold Zweig, Lion Feuchtwanger, Franz Werfel, Erich Kästner, Robert Musil and Joseph Roth, as well as many more. Their books will disappear from public libraries. Countless other international works of literature, philosophy and silence will also be condemned in this way, along with the complete works of Heinrich Heine, who once said: "Where they have burned books, they will end in burning human beings."

Students pile books to be burned onto a lorry.

The Parliament in flames. Communist suspect executed after sensationalist trial

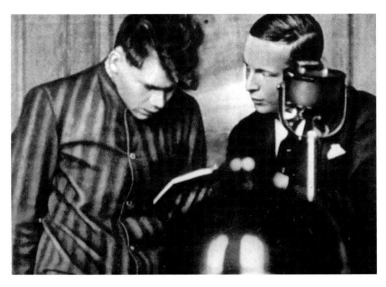

On the night of February 27, much of the parliament building, whose first stone had been laid by Emperor Wilhelm I on 9 June 1886, is destroyed by fire.

Marinus van der Lubbe, a Dutch communist, is arrested as a suspect at the scene of the crime. A wave of arrests follows, practically all involving members of the KPD (German initials for the German Communist Party). At the flame-engulfed parliament itself, Adolf Hitler announces that the Communists are to blame for the fire. The truth is, however, that many are convinced that the Nazis themselves started the blaze for propaganda purposes.

The parliament building burns down.

10 January 1934: "...Van der Lubbe, who set fire to the parliament, was executed this morning" (Report from the German Office of Information).

What is the future that awaits Berlin?

An epilogue with a warning

Interior view of the
Reichstag dome.

Berlin: what a state to get into!

After the city was brutally divided into two sectors, US president John F. Kennedy proclaimed: "Ich bin ein Berliner". In doing so, he did not refer to a geographic place of origin, but to a feeling. What this city can mean to each separate individual has never been solely to do with its citizens, its buildings, its woods and its lakes. For more than a hundred years, this unique city has been synonymous with opening up to the world, resurgence and progress, courage, lust for life, tolerance and a sharp, fresh sense of humour. And thanks to these enormous attractions, Berlin continues to be one of the world's most popular destinations for visitors. There is always something happening here. In most cases, more than anywhere else, night and day, with very different events in each of Berlin's 23 districts. Everything is still as constantly-changing, thrilling and exciting as ever. Here, life is both shaped and shared by more than 450,000 foreigners from 183 different nationalities. Recent decades have also seen the growth and expansion of the "ecological" ideas born in the 1970s about cultural diversity sustained by opinion makers who even flew against the prejudices rife in the little world of Berlin's autochthonous citizens. Nowadays, many are quick to point out that in Berlin, has happened long before in New York, London and Paris, "parallel societies" have sprung up amongst the huge communities of immigrants.

Those most fearful and pessimistic predict that all attempts to foster our moral values amongst these "new Berliners" are doomed to abject failure. And they back up their arguments with such clichés as: "a bridge does not reduce the distance between the two banks". This is a metaphor that cannot, in itself, be refuted. On the other hand, those in favour of multiculturalism argue that differences in lifestyles should not be "smoothed out", so that everyone is the same, but understood, as anything else would resemble a kind of forced evangelism. What is different should be made accessible and easy to understand, for ignorance and fear are the roots of all evil.

Neither do the inhibitions that are spreading amongst immigrant communities, rising crime rates and the brutalisation that is spreading quickly under the veneer of religious conviction and shady ideas about honour encourage people to see things differently. On the contrary, the representatives from the different nationalities and religious communities present in Berlin need to find ways and means to transmit what might be seen as higher ethical values, an image of humanity and the world free from nationalist exaltation and fundamentalist conviction. Berlin, a veritable breeding ground for different models for alternative lifestyles, could also be called upon to establish a few rules in this regard. Precisely due to the background provided by German history, which reached its terrible climax in Berlin, the city could well provide a successful, tried-and-tested model for the future integration of immigrants, an example of unsurpassed importance. Our country probably owes the world such an effort, but there can be no doubt that it owes it to itself.

Berlin is famed more than ever amongst creative young people, who flock here from all over the world. And for the second time (the first was in the 1920s), the city is becoming a renowned "gateway to the East", a platform for European cultural and intellectual connections. Just as occurred after the October Revolution in Russia in 1917, Berlin's Russian community is now formed by more than 100,000 people and, just as in those times, Russian intellectuals have opened numerous art galleries and cultural centres. And literary circles and debates are returning, just as in Imperial times. Whilst, right beside them, we discover, breathless, futurist laboratories experimenting with a view to times to come.

With regard to the economic scene, the main centre around which East-West European relations revolves is spinning ever more quickly, more colourfully, attracting to itself ever more amazed, expectant, joyful and courageous participants. A key area here is the vast, growing service sector, which is acquiring more and more importance. Alongside London and Milan, and just behind Paris, Berlin could soon become a veritable fashion capital, as the city had never boasted so many design and production studios as now. Today, Berlin's development is without doubt the most extraordinary the city has enjoyed in the last hundred years. This flourishing period will give birth to something completely new to the city of Berlin. Anyone worried about the future should remember that the everything and its opposite is possible in the future. A clear example of this is that the risks to all of us are becoming increasingly greater, whilst the opportunities are also growing at a similar rate.

An attractive, flourishing future

Balzac's novel *Illusions perdues* (Lost Illusions) is the tale of an ambitious young man from a small provincial town in the outskirts of Paris who is in a great hurry to make a name for himself: amongst women, in society, at the stock exchange, in the press, in politics... The possibilities offered by great cities are endless, and there have always been young people like Balzac's Lucien, sure of themselves and convinced that provincial clocks tick round too slowly to enable one's ingenuity to develop at the proper rate. It has always been so, and it will always be so. Berlin knows many such immigrants who have sought their fortunes here, and found it. Even today, even at this very minute, the leading caravan of the successful continues to enter the city.

Despite all this, Berlin lacks the architectural harmony of Rome, it is not infused with the *pathos* of Rome that links worlds and epochs. In comparison with such cities Berlin's tradition are sprinkled with but little of the patina age as yet. Even so, the "gates" of Berlin are wide open to all those who have questions to ask of all the brave and daring, as no other great city in the world. That has been the Berlin way since the times of Frederick the Great. And with good reasons; precisely the permanent imperfection and endless contradictions of this city, which neither finds calm, nor does it wish to find such a thing.

Berliners, before the history of their city

It is never an easy task to summarise the history of a city, how it was formed and its lifestyle, much less when the subject is an intense, agitated story of love and pain such as, for example, the history of Berlin. This is a city that has been vanquished, conquered and occupied as often as other cities, but asphyxiated, walled in, like no other. The sequences of historic events that have taken place is completely believable, and not only the worse aspects. Those "pens for hire" type writers who narrate fables whilst reined in, restricted, by their close relationship, their vassal status, with regard to intellectual princes, kings, dictators and rulers, have left us description that attempt to attract their future readers to the side of those who gave them their bread. And those able to write their chronicles in more fortunate conditions of total freedom from corruption took no little information from sources with vested interests. Just how controversial are the ways in which surviving direct witnesses have seen Berlin's history in recent histories has been amply demonstrated by terrible occurrences, firstly in May 1945 and once again in November 1989.

The ability to sell one's own shadow

Berliners have always been optimistic people. But over the last fifteen years, reality has once more brought fear to many of them (as to most Germans in general). At the end of the Second World War and after German Reunification, millions of people became "turncoats", abandoning or denying their devastating convictions, covering up or reneging on their personal biographies.

Historic events become twisted. The truth is silenced and manipulated, bent to serve particular interests and desires.
Perhaps even most of those who lived in the Soviet occupation zone and became adults in the GDR today lead surprisingly "shadowless" lives. Since 1990, in their progress towards freedom, they have thrown off part of their identity, which may well be considered faithful, as if it were useless ballast, to increase their rhythm and speed of life, once more aerodynamic, streamlined. This image reminds us to a certain extent of the fable in which a man sells his soul to the devil, and with it his shadow. At heart, this is a metaphor that could be used to describe countless periods in human history, wherever people's very identity is mutilated, with the addition of a chapter of life ripped out, still warm and alive, impregnated with guilt from which expiation is impossible.

The postwar generation owe little to their fathers and grandfathers

The generation of fathers who built their "workers' and farmers' state" has little today to teach, what we might call "leaving their children to pay. And much the same can also be said of the generation of parents in West Germany who achieved the "economic miracle" of the 1950s thanks to aid received under the Marshall Plan and which they "milked" from the Western Allies.

Whilst the GDR – economically exploited by the Soviets – was established in part of Berlin, West Berliners, during the coldest period of their lives, held onto democracy as if it were an article of warm clothing. But over the next twenty years, for most people, this was too far away and for some for a long period of time. Simply, it did not make them strong enough. Moving with imagination, even with the apparent security of the huge progress, many came to grief on the rocks of complex and numerous training possibilities. It is always the same: the weakest in spirit need support. For "marble is nothing without the sculptor".

After the mid-1960s, the sons and daughters who had gradually become angry, began to resist the return of fears that they considered had become a thing of the past. And ever since, their parents, preening themselves proudly, believing that these young people owed them freedom and wellbeing, have had to put up with terribly embarrassing questions. One such question, one which went straight to the central nervous system was and still is that which affects the non-existing sense of guilt amongst those who are awash in blame.

Was it not the most humble obligation of this older generation to silently put to one side the rubble of their abandoned responsibilities?
Could they not merely do the necessary without boasting about it?
And was it not a terrible sign of sinister cruelty, this act of charging into their children's account this damned fulfilment of obligations?
And is not the dishonour that attaches to part of the elder generation in the form of their boasts much crueller, the greater the torment that we perceive amongst the more than six million children, women, old folk and men who were tortured in German concentration camps, gassed, shot, beaten to death, and whose remains, buried and scattered by the wind, have been left to "materialise", unlike the rubble of the bombed houses of the authors of such crimes?
Yes, the older generation did not lose, bloated with pride, after it was demonstrated to them that they no longer had any heart, also the last remaining crumbs of credibility when calls began to be heard for praise to be heaped on their "recovery"?
And, moreover, was not their vanity dented (even when this can be vaunted with evident discretion) by addition the identity of those who, in silence or with a low whispering, attempted to oppose the terrible obligations of acting of the mass that was heading for the abyss?

What is the future that awaits Berlin?

Because these secret heroes, their names unknown to anyone now, did really exist. Free thinkers who survived the war with their hands clean but have been engulfed by the spirit of collective guilt.

The only chance in history

Young Berliners, somewhere between coming of age and the leap into a professional career, and young people living in Germany generally, have no reason to be ashamed about the links that bind them to their fathers' and grandfathers' generations. But if they were not enormously affected by the devastating mistakes and terrible acts that earlier generations are guilty of, now, decades after those events, never to be forgotten, they would be taking onto themselves actions and omissions that are no so much less serious and, therefore, could not be free from the corresponding reproaches and blame.

For those with their future still ahead of them, remembering what happened is, without doubt, one of the noblest obligations that a person can take upon themselves. Merely by facing the ghosts of the past, people can justify their hopes and chances for the future.

Memorial sites built in the country over the last few decades are essential and will continue to be so. The expressiveness and feeling imbued in such commemorative sites, and also the consolation that they offer, mark out the path, making the human greatness of the mourner part of their construction. Here, the sufferer becomes an intrinsic part of the place. Devoted to the greatest and most terrible crime in the history of humanity, near the Brandenburg Gate: the Holocaust Memorial. The inhumanity of the pseudo-communist postwar GDR regime continues to be present for us, particularly in such commemorative memorial sites as the former *Staatssicherheit* (Ministry for State Security, Stasi) prison in Hohenschönhausen.

Holocaust Memorial:

Field of blocks designed by Peter Eisenman as the central feature of this commemorative monument in the former ministerial gardens.

The former Berlin-Hohenschönhausen remand prison, run by the Ministry for State Security.

View of the so-called "submarine", the underground cell section. The prison was reopened as a memorial centre on 22 December 1995.

In 1963, the Wall Museum was opened at Checkpoint Charlie, the most infamous border post in the world, to commemorate the courage of the civilians who jumped over the inhuman walls, their faith and hope, but also to remind us of the deepest needs people can feel and the most terrible way in which they can be divided. The museum was established by Rainer Hildebrandt, a fighter for freedom persecuted by the Nazis and run by August 13 Organisation that he himself founded, and which takes its name from the date the Wall began to be built. After Hildebrandt's death in January 2004), in an act of intrepid calm and serenity before all obstacles, including political intrigue, and against vague indifference, the museum was saved for the future by his widow, Alexandra Hildebrandt.

The legendary Wall Museum at Checkpoint Charlie.

191

What is the future that awaits Berlin?

Berlin looks to the future

Just as little as New York represents the United States of America, so incompletely is Germany reflected in Berlin. If, for example, we lament the until now unpredictable risks posed by the European Union, due to the exception conditions here, this city enjoys special status, including a vast range of privileges. Since the EU was established, the business landscape has changed drastically. On the one hand, the national climate has become more rarefied due, particularly, to drastically high tax levels and relatively high salaries. On the other, the business situation has improved almost without limit due to the fact that enormous facilities are provided to allow companies to chose the most appropriate site on which to establish their production centres. Although wages may be low, taxes are also low, the unions' teeth have been drawn, and even the political climate is favourable to business.

Subversive movements are set up, and these soon demand maximum flexibility from qualified German businessmen. They also have to make their living outside the country. They will become the Nomads of the Third Millennium: mass movements comparable to the migrations of earlier times may take place. More people than ever, from all over Europe, are making Berlin their life centre. Over the next 15-20 years, the city's population will, in all probability, reach 4.5 million inhabitants (the current population is around 3.4 million). For even more people, then, Berlin will become the way station that will mobilise all their energy with its magnetic, luminous attraction. And it may be that it will finally develop its own personality, as most of the potential that exists here, geographically and materially, in the human and in the spiritual, remains perfectly intact.

As a first generation, today's young people have the chance to live various lives one after another or even at the same time. This is a chance that many will lament, but those able to savour and enjoy it will see this opportunity as a privilege. Though it is true that there have never been as many confused, disoriented people as there are today, at the same time, each individual enjoys freedom of thought, desire and action of which their predecessors could not even have dreamed.

"The future belongs to those who believe in the beauty of their dreams"

Eleanor Roosevelt